D0837787

Recovering a Public Vision for Public Television

CRITICAL MEDIA STUDIES
INSTITUTIONS, POLITICS, AND CULTURE

Series Editor
Andrew Calabrese, University of Colorado

Advisory Board
Patricia Aufderheide, American University • Jean-Claude Burgelman, Free University of Brussels • Simone Chambers, University of Toronto • Nicholas Garnham, University of Westminster • Hanno Hardt, University of Iowa • Gay Hawkins, The University of New South Wales • Maria Heller, Eötvös Loránd University • Robert Horwitz, University of California at San Diego • Douglas Kellner, University of California at Los Angeles • Gary Marx, Massachusetts Institute of Technology • Toby Miller, New York University • Vincent Mosco, Carleton University • Janice Peck, University of Colorado • Manjunath Pendakur, Southern Illinois University • Arvind Rajagopal, New York University • Kevin Robins, Goldsmiths College • Saskia Sassen, University of Chicago • Colin Sparks, University of Westminster • Slavko Splichal, University of Ljubljana • Thomas Streeter, University of Vermont • Liesbet van Zoonen, University of Amsterdam • Janet Wasko, University of Oregon

VCTC Library
Hartness Library
Vermont Technical College
Randolph Center, VT 05061

Recovering a Public Vision for Public Television

Glenda R. Balas

ROWMAN & LITTLEFIELD PUBLISHERS, INC.
Lanham • Boulder • New York • Oxford

ROWMAN & LITTLEFIELD PUBLISHERS, INC.

Published in the United States of America
by Rowman & Littlefield Publishers, Inc.
A Member of the Rowman & Littlefield Publishing Group
4501 Forbes Boulevard, Suite 200, Lanham, Maryland 20706
www.rowmanlittlefield.com

PO Box 317, Oxford OX2 9RU, United Kingdom

Copyright © 2003 by Rowman & Littlefield Publishers, Inc.

All rights reserved. No part of this publication may be reproduced, stored in a retrieval system, or transmitted in any form or by any means, electronic, mechanical, photocopying, recording, or otherwise, without the prior permission of the publisher.

British Library Cataloguing in Publication Information Available

Library of Congress Cataloging-in-Publication Data

Balas, Glenda R., 1949–
    Recovering a public vision for public television / Glenda R. Balas
        p. cm.—(Critical media studies)
Includes bibliographical references and index.
    ISBN 0-7425-2386-1 (cloth : alk. paper)—ISBN 0-7425-2387-X (pbk. : alk. paper)
    1. Public television—United States. 2. Pressure groups—United States. 3. Corporate sponsorship—United States. I. Title. II. Series.

    HE8700.79 .B35 2003
    384.55'4'0973—dc21

                                                                  2002012258

Printed in the United States of America

♾™ The paper used in this publication meets the minimum requirements of American National Standard for Information Sciences—Permanence of Paper for Printed Library Materials, ANSI/NISO Z39.48-1992.

For Sam Becker and Bruce Gronbeck

Contents

Acknowledgments

Many people helped me with this book. The project began with graduate papers for seminars in the Communication Studies Department at the University of Iowa and evolved into dissertation research. I am especially grateful for the help of John Peters, who urged me to ask the larger questions; Bruce Gronbeck, who encouraged me to explore the small texts; and Sam Becker, who offered the insider perspective of one involved in the broadcast reform movement of the 1950s. Kathleen Farrell introduced me to archival research; Eric Rothenbuhler's insights are woven throughout the book; and Ken Cmiel's own fine academic writing provided inspiration. All have been good friends and exemplary role models in my teaching and research. I am deeply appreciative.

At Rowman & Littlefield Publishers, I am indebted to Andrew Calabrese, the Critical Media Studies series editor, for his interest in the project. I am also grateful to Brenda Hadenfeldt, production editor Alden Perkins, and copyeditor Glenn Wright for their able assistance in preparing the book for publication. I have also greatly appreciated the encouragement of my colleagues at the University of New Mexico, and I am especially grateful to Robert Avery and Richard Schaefer, who read final versions of the manuscript.

I received an American Fellow Dissertation Award from the American Association of University Women; the Moody Research Grant from the Lyndon Baines Johnson Presidential Library; the Sidney J. Weinberg Research Fellowship from the Franklin and Eleanor Roosevelt Institute; a research grant-in-aid from the Harry S. Truman Presidential Library; and Indiana University's Everett Helm Research Fellowship. I also received a summer research grant from DePauw University, which allowed me to revise my original manuscript for publication. I could not have completed the work without this funding.

Nor could I have finished the project without the ongoing support of my family. My parents and siblings provided wise (and humorous) counsel throughout the research and writing stages of this book. Heather Wellborn Balas and Jason Christopher Balas, now grown children with lives of their own, have always supported their mother's projects; this one was no exception.

And, finally, I acknowledge the very important role that my colleagues in public TV have played in the conception and completion of this book. Duane Ryan and other professionals at KENW-TV in Portales, New Mexico, in particular, taught me to expect the best of public television.

Introduction

> Stephen is eight years old. [He] is tiny, desperate, unwell. Some-
> times he talks to himself. He moves his mouth as if he were talk-
> ing. At other times he laughs out loud in class for no apparent rea-
> son. He is also an indescribably mild and unmalicious child. He
> cannot do his school work very well.
>
> —Jonathan Kozol, *Death at an Early Age*

Writing in 1967, Jonathan Kozol described a young black student bat-
tling to survive in the inner city schools of Boston. Twenty-five years
later, Kozol reported that the schools for America's poor were even
worse. Inadequately staffed, segregated, and violent, they were also un-
safe and unclean. Their students faced low reading scores, high
dropout rates, poor motivation, and worries about being caught alone
under the stairs or in the rest room (Kozol 1991: 5). And although Kozol praised the strong families and teachers of inner city schools in his
1998 essay "Principals, Grandmothers, and Resiliency," the incidence
of poverty, hunger, segregation, and physical illness for these students
is overwhelming (Kozol 1998: 20-23). A 2001 report by the Josephson
Institute of Ethics reported that more than one third of students said
they did not feel safe at school, while one in five high school males reported carrying a weapon to school (2001). Recent data suggest that
52 percent of fourth-graders in Mississippi and California can't read at

grade level, that one in three Hispanic students drops out before completing high school, and that one million American teenagers become pregnant each year ("America's Forgotten Children" 2002: 1; "Dropout Rates" 2002: 1; A. Robertson 1998: 4). The United States has the highest youth homicide rate among the world's 26 wealthiest nations, and suicide is the third leading cause of death among American adolescents ("National Education News" 2000: 2; "Suicide in the United States" 2002: 1). America's youth are in a state of crisis.

The challenge facing U.S. children stands as one example of America's need for media that promote a just and healthy society by helping citizens address important social problems. Clearly, the issues facing youth at school, at home, and on the streets are not the sole responsibility of public broadcasting. A multitude of individuals and groups must shoulder the burden and the blame for a society that places many children at risk, and solving these problems will require participation by us all. At the same time, public broadcasting, built on the rhetoric of serving the public interest, could legitimately be expected to intervene creatively on behalf of kids at the margins. Instead, the system's efforts to change the lives and opportunities of poor, homeless, and troubled youngsters have been minimal; programs for children have been limited largely to school-centered instructional programming.

Public television's failure to construct itself as an agent of public talk and social reform has been exacerbated by its alignment with the goals and practices of commercial broadcasting. This affiliation with market-driven media alters public media's form and function and makes it vulnerable to attack, especially by those who would eliminate public funding. Even more critically, the absence of an institutional identity built on shared public goals and a powerful sense of its own history precludes public television from moving with confidence in the American social landscape. A system that has become increasingly timid, oriented to the bottom line, and victimized by internal struggle and infighting, public service broadcasting falters in a complicated, competitive media environment. Working without a coherent vision rooted in original purposes, public media professionals grapple with diminishing viewership, insufficient resources, and a marginalized position for public media in the larger culture. As Patricia Aufderheide observed in 1991, public television was once the sole source for the "safely splendid," in-depth public affairs programs, and quality children's shows (176). Now PBS vies with a range of niche services for the audiences once considered public TV's core constituency. In addition, that public TV offers few programs for ethnic minorities, working people, teenagers, the elderly, rural America, and community activists further narrows public broadcasting's audience and brings into question its claim that it provides programs for all Americans. Public television is seen as an alternative and peripheral text, operating at the edges of American social life. Lacking a unifying public vision—and seemingly complacent in keeping it that way—U.S. public broadcasting enters the twenty-first century as a shadow of the democratic media system its founders envisioned.

Public television's failure to achieve its potential as democratic media does not mean that the system has always worked without a vision. Indeed, public broadcasting has long been viewed as capable of invigorating important national discourses and functioning as an agent of social change. Its earliest leaders were champions of public speech, participatory democracy, and the use of broadcasting to solve common problems. These public media visionaries included Judge Ira Robinson, who said radio was the "greatest implement of democracy yet given to mankind" (1930: 3); Richard Hull, who in a 1979 interview with Jim Robertson called noncommercial broadcasting a "social dream" (Hull Papers, 5/6/13, box 1); and Raymond Hurlbert, who employed education as social reform in the early 1960s:

> The urban areas in the state [of Alabama] had fine school systems but the rural systems in Alabama were handicapped because the better qualified teachers gravitated to the urban centers. The schools in the rural areas were not only handicapped from talent but from funds. Many did not have full terms of school each year. Certain counties of the state would start school early in the summer and then turn school out in the fall for cotton picking.
>
> The cry, and the very plausible argument that I presented to the members of the legislature and to all of the groups to which I spoke, was that equal opportunity was going to be enhanced in such a way that the people in the poor and the deprived areas of the state not only should have but they *must* have the access to the best that there is. And that every child in Alabama was entitled to the best. (Hurlbert 1981)

Like FCC Commissioner Frieda Hennock, who led the fight for reserved educational channels in the fifties, these individuals were committed to public service broadcasting—a television system that acted in the public interest, cultivated community involvement, and supported excellence in education, communication, and the creative arts. All pursued the vision that public broadcasting could invigorate discussion, engage a working democracy, and promote cultural diversity as a staple of American life. Like public-sphere scholars Hannah Arendt, John Dewey, and Jürgen Habermas, these founders of public broadcasting desired the creation of a modern polis that could transform private people into active citizens with commitments to public life. Although the history texts of American broadcasting have largely ignored these social, intellectual, and philosophic commitments, the actual spoken and written discourse of many early public media advocates offers significant evidence of a coherent, collectively understood, and accepted sense of vision.

In order to understand how public media's institutional vision dissolved over time, I examine three key moments in which public broadcasting not only commanded a national audience, but engaged in a vigorous struggle for resources. During these historical moments—the Wagner-Hatfield Amendment in 1934, the FCC allocations of 1950–51, and the Public Broadcasting Act of 1967—the philosophy and structure of nonprofit media took center stage; and the national conversation turned to issues of spectrum control, educational reform, and popular community. Despite the promise of the moment, however, broadcast reformers fumbled, hedged, and compromised. Making choices in 1934, 1950–51, and 1967 that maintained the status quo, their chances for increased resources and greater social influence slipped away. The Great Depression, the Red Scare, and the 1960s each provided a rich and complicated social landscape in which to debate democratic media. Even more importantly, each also challenged public media to action, to hone its vision of service through service. In each instance, the road taken abdicated public media's responsibility as change agent and narrowed the public sphere.

The critique that public broadcasting acts without a compelling mission is not uncommon. Communication scholars and PTV professionals alike argue that a lack of institutional purpose prevents public TV from moving with accomplishment in American social life. Former PBS president Larry Grossman, for example, has maintained that public television's lack of mission not only dooms it to second-class status, without mechanisms to make timely program decisions, but also keeps the system at war with itself (Sucherman 1987: 68). James Day (1995: 4), former general manager of WNET/New York, bemoans PTV's "vanished vision" of comprehensive and diverse service; and Robert Avery (Avery and Pepper 1980: 126) and Williard Rowland (1993: 191)—media scholars who have analyzed public broadcasting policy for decades—have argued the system acts only as a "palliative" to the weaknesses of commercial broadcasting. William Hoynes (1994: 154) points to public television's marginalized status in the United States and to critics' charges that the system is obsolescent.

Even the popular press has brought a critical eye to public TV practice. A drawing by nationally syndicated cartoonist Pat Oliphant in the October 1987 issue of *Channels* magazine depicted a desert scene populated only by two vultures, an iguana, and a spindly-legged, unshaven beggar wearing nothing but a diaper and a sign that read, "PBS, Lost, Please Help" (Oliphant 69). The cartoon's critique of public TV as a bewildered and lost soul in America's "Great Wastelands" was echoed the same year by PBS producer Stuart Sucherman, who characterized public television as an "unfocused underachiever . . . [that] doesn't work" (Sucherman 1987: 68). Ten years later, outside consultants called in to help unify PTV would offer a similar view. BMR Associates observed in 1996:

> Public television is neither a single institution nor a community, [and] as time has passed, [its] sense of national purpose has slowly eroded. . . . As a result, local licensees feel less responsibility for the welfare of the national phenomenon we know as public television.
>
> In the past, certain external forces—most notably, the almost universal need for federal support—exerted a steadying and unifying force. The threatened absence of federal funding as a unifying issue exposes PTV's underlying instability. ("PTV" 1996: 17)

Like William Hoynes, Robert Avery, Alan Stavitsky, Tom McCourt, James Day, James Ledbetter, and Jerrold Starr, I am critical of the lackluster record of public media practice within U.S. culture. Like Williard Rowland, I worry that its lack of vision binds public broadcasting to a perpetual and debilitating state of mediocrity: "U.S. public broadcasting is nowhere near as significant a force as it ought be and yet, internally, it is remarkably quiescent on that score. . . . [T]he institution has no internal gyroscope—no fire in the belly, and no willingness to challenge the stultifying forces that surround and seduce it" (Rowland 1993: 190). In addition, an in-depth exploration of the social-historical environments and primary documents related to three of the most important events in U.S. public media history can advance a progressive critique of public media practice.

This book explores long-term problems associated with the failed institutional vision for public television, and offers an integrated approach to public media practice, suggesting that democratic media are defined by 1) an allegiance to engaged public talk; 2) the use of broadcasting to advance social reform; and 3) efforts to cultivate a broad-based, popular community. Chapter 1 looks at public TV's original public mission and leads us into the three historical cases. Chapter 2 explores the struggles for radio spectrum space in the 1930s, specifically the debates surrounding the Wagner-Hatfield Amendment and Section 307(c) of the Communications Act of 1934. These public battles for control of the U.S. airwaves pitted for-profit interests against noncommercial broadcasters, who lost their spectrum holdings, in part due to campaign disorganization and failed commitments to popular voices.

Chapter 3 discusses how the culture of domesticity and a fearful national mood, coupled with rhetorical strategies that limited speakers and audience to the mainstream, defined the shape and narrowed the scope of U.S. noncommercial television in the 1950s. The educational model—tied to values of privacy, home, service to children, and national security—acted to constrain the public potential of noncommercial broadcasting. Chapter 4 shows that public television's promise in community-building was cut short in the 1960s by the system's lack of commitment to neighborhood discourses and grassroots democracy. Framed by the social and cultural agenda of the Ford Foundation and the high federalism of LBJ's Great Society, public TV abandoned its early roots in local performance, becoming not an advocate for community but an "expert voice." The conclusion offers a program for public media work designed to perform public service and restore public practices. Addressing ways public television can develop as a national institution of publicness, it presents six concepts that may work to enable the public speech of American constituencies, build inclusive communities, and employ broadcasting as a change agent.

The absence of a deep, enduring, and systemic support for public life has brought with it compromises that cost public broadcasting not only key resources, but also its identity and institutional purpose. The losses of 1934, 1950–51, and 1967 jeopardized public broadcasting's sense of itself, and the organization that survives today is almost un-recognizable as the public service–oriented medium begun in the 1920s. Public broadcasters must not only acknowledge and pursue the use of broadcasting to further the public good, they must recognize that the recovery of public mission for U.S. public media requires its reconstitution through altered practice. By drawing on discursive re-sources of the past and by forming a commitment to viable civic ac-tion in the present, public broadcasting can perform as an agent of public purpose.

Working to redeem public media's founding visions and to bring out previously unacknowledged but implicit arguments for publicness, this book adds to the body of arguments justifying financial support and bold initiatives for public broadcasting in the United States and abroad. It is my hope that it will contribute usefully to the growing conversation about media reform in the United States. Central to this work are beliefs that community is helped, not hindered, by the mul-tivocal diversity of American life, and that public media, reinvigo-rated and adequately funded, could level the discursive playing field for the unvoiced and less powerful. I have been guided by a vision ar-ticulated by Richard Hull near the end of his career as a broadcast reformer and early leader of public television:

> I think we were builders. We had to be. . . . Somehow I got all steamed up on "everybody should know more"; you get that way, I think, at an A & M College or University . . . Wisconsin is both. . . . the Land Grant tradition. . . . It wasn't anything I did . . . it wasn't other than the nor-mal vanities, money or prestige—that makes me sound too darn pious; of course, there was a drive for recognition and vanity. But I believed . . . that if everybody knew all there is to know, it would be a great step for-ward. (Hull Papers, 5/6/13, box 1)

Newton Minnow (1993: xii) has suggested that the international pub-lic broadcasting environment has changed radically over the last decade, and that the "new game cannot be played by the old rules." If the old rules no longer apply, the old visions surely do.

CHAPTER ONE

Glide Path to Extinction: Consequences of a Failed Public Mission

In a move that garnered press coverage across the country, Congresswoman Nita Lowey (D-N.Y.) announced two surprise witnesses and held up hand puppets of Bert and Ernie during a House Appropriations subcommittee hearing in January 1995. "Make no mistake about it," she said. "This debate is about Big Bird and Oscar the Grouch and Barney and Kermit and the new Republican majority that would put them on the chopping block" (qtd. in Gray 1995: A22). Framed in the metaphors of *Sesame Street* and cast as a partisan street fight, the 1995–96 battle over federal funds for public broadcasting had begun.

The next eighteen months would produce a colorful national debate about public broadcasting that stretched from Washington to the Internet and talk radio and involved thousands of Americans. As House Speaker Newt Gingrich called public TV the "sandbox of the rich" and vowed to "zero out" the Corporation for Public Broadcasting (CPB), House Democrats Lowey, Nancy Pelosi (California), and Ed Markey (Massachusetts) held a press conference to show off 35,000 postcards in support of public broadcasting from viewers around the country (Edwards 1995b: C1). Their congressional aides, decked out in rented Bert and Ernie costumes, delivered the postcards around Capitol Hill (Brenner 1995: 1). CPB board chairman Henry Cauthen called the threatened budget cuts a "death blow" to the system (Edwards and Trescott 1995: C1); PBS president Ervin Duggin likened a commercialized public television to Thomas Hardy's "ruined maid" (Kolbert 1995: C1); and a poll conducted by Opinion Research Corporation of Princeton, N.J., showed that 84 percent of Americans favored either current or increased levels of federal support for public TV (Rathbun 1995: 164). In the Clinton administration's first public statement about the controversy on March 2, 1995, Vice President Al Gore blamed Republican "extremists" for an "all-out mean-spirited attack" on PBS and then donned a Mister Rogers cardigan to discuss the merits of public TV with 40 preschoolers (Edwards 1995c: C1). Constituents of Senator James Longley (R-Maine) protested his anti-PBS stance by demonstrating in Big Bird and Cookie Monster suits; and public television fundraisers adopted the on-air slogan, "If PBS doesn't do it, who else will?"

Larry Pressler, Republican senator from South Dakota and chair of the Senate Interstate Commerce Committee, made the front page of the *New York Times* when he advocated privatization of public broadcasting and suggested that Nickelodeon should produce PBS kids' shows (Edwards 1995a: A1). Telecommunications conglomerates Bell Atlantic and Jones Intercable immediately expressed interest in buying public television stations, provoking outrage among public broadcasting supporters that the system "could be sold off for scrap to the highest commercial bidder" (Edwards 1995a: C1).

It was a moment marked by high-pitched hyperbole, political partisanship, and public incredulity that a media system so entrenched in American cultural life could face extinction. Columnist George Will's admonition to "give them the ax" (1995: C1) flew in the face of grassroots support for noncommercial broadcasting, and after receiving "bags of mail" from constituents even Newt Gingrich softened his stance. An initial call to zero out funding within three years, with reductions of 33 percent each year, eventually evolved into federal allocations for public television of $285.6 million in 1995, $275 million in 1996, $260 million in 1997, and $250 million in 1998. Some industry observers suggested an annual funding level of $250 million would continue well into the twenty-first century. Others, like David Brugger, president of America's Public Television Stations (APTS), were less optimistic, predicting a "glide path to zero" (see Blandenbaker 1996: 1). Even so, level funding was expected to last until 2002, providing U.S. public broadcasters time to "learn self-sufficiency" and to chart a plan to replace the 14.6 percent of its budget funded at that time by federal allocation (PBS 1996d: 1).

In the fall of 1996—as the country readied itself for the 1996 presidential election and PBS put a brand new season on the air—catastrophe, it would seem, had been averted. Public broadcasting had been given time to get its affairs in order. As a *Washington Post* headline announced, Big Bird had been "Taken Off Death Row" (Farhi 1995: C1).

Early Visions and Visionaries

Officially established in 1967 as a national broadcasting service, public television's 125 original stations held in common general commitments to education, community, and, especially for those affiliated with Midwestern universities, the land-grant tradition. As descendants of educational radio—which had its own origins in the broadcast reform movement of the late 1920s and early 1930s—these stations were veterans of bitter struggles for spectrum space and capital. Their managers had taken the stand numerous times to defend noncommercial broadcasting before congressional committees, the Federal Communications Commission (FCC), and university presidents. People who had passed through the fire together, early public TV professionals had uncommon friendships with one another, and many careers developed in an informal mentoring system that passed myth, knowledge, spirit, and history from one generation to the next. These men and women formed professional organizations—the National Committee on Education by Radio, Joint Committee on Educational Television, National Association of Educational Broadcasters, and Educational Television Stations—and they organized and attended seminars on noncommercial broadcasting, most notably at the University of Illinois's Allerton House and Ohio State University. In 1955, years before ETV telephone or satellite interconnection, educational broadcasters developed a tape library and an interdependent "bicycle" system of distribution. If not a network, then surely these early stations were a family, bound together by interpersonal relationships and a history of struggle, social and professional commitment, and the desire to survive.

Even with the cohesiveness of collective memory (coupled with national legislative sanction in 1967) early U.S. noncommercial broadcasting failed to articulate a formal statement of institutional purpose. Over the years, despite an increase from 125 stations in 1967 to 347 in 2003, and a significant technological upgrade of the system as a whole, public television has continued to work without an official mandate arrived at through industry consensus, government edict, or even popular opinion. There has been no charter, no constitution, no plan by which public TV could position itself as an institution of the American mass media. This is not to suggest that the system has always worked without a semblance of a vision. Although lacking a formal mission statement, many early public broadcasters were nonetheless united in their belief that radio and television should enable public speech, community attachments, and democratic practice. The history texts of American broadcasting have ignored most of these men and women, but their spoken and written discourses offer proof of a coherent, collectively understood, and accepted sense of public purpose. The chapters that follow seek to reclaim the central tenets of that vision in building a public media ideology based on concepts of publicness, community, and cultural diversity.

Public television has lost sight of its historic underpinnings and moved further into market-driven media economics, not only seeking private funding but accepting capitalists' indicators of success. This affiliation with the market and the loss of its democratic promise makes public television vulnerable to attack, seen dramatically in the 1995–96 congressional debate over funding. Further, the absence of a clearly stated and commonly understood mission has cost public television its sense of institutional selfhood and a broad-based engagement with the American people. To rally around Big Bird in time of financial peril should not be confused with the purposeful employment of public media to improve social life. Without a passion for public work by public television and the American people, public TV will continue to flounder on the sidelines. Its great potential to invigorate national discourse and to function as a principal player in America's social, political, and artistic quests will remain tragically unrealized. There is much at stake in the reformulation of a powerful purpose for public TV, including creating a protected space for robust public talk and decision making. Lacking commitments to the theories and practices of publicness and a healthy disdain for the pollution of capitalist media, however, the system cannot deliver.

Public Broadcasting and the Public Sphere

Acknowledging U.S. public media's failing sense of collective purpose, the Twentieth Century Fund sponsored a task force in 1993 to study the future of public TV. It concluded that the mission of public television should be the "enrichment and strengthening of American society and culture" through high-quality national programming. The task force advocated structural change to eliminate both overlapping services and federal funds for stations. Strong national programs and an expanded educational service were seen as public television's proper contribution to American social life (Twentieth Century Fund 1993: 4–6).

This was a controversial report, in large part because of its call to eliminate federal funding for stations. Also problematic, however, was the document's lack of support for the practice and theories of public life. Public broadcasting's foundations are democratic; the system's underpinnings are tied to public speech, access to governance, and community. The task force's report did not address these critical concepts of participatory democracy, but rather offered up a statement of strategy about economics and the production of an elite text. This position stands in marked contrast to the words of Dick Hull, a pioneer in public broadcasting whose thirty-year career distinguished him as a leading voice of public TV. In an oral history interview with Jim Robertson conducted just months before his death in 1980, Hull spoke of public TV's mission as a "social dream": "I think one of the reasons that the sense of mission is gone is because nobody was teaching sense of mission, and those on the mission were too busy doing it" (Hull Papers, 5/6/13, box 1). The passion of a "social dream" and the needs of American people to speak—and be heard—in matters of the everyday are not a part of the Twentieth Century Fund report. Nor are theoretical constructs that can be employed in developing a commonly understood mission for public TV. As we begin the hard work of articulating an identity and purpose for U.S. public media, theories of the public sphere can provide useful support.

Theoretical Foundations of Publicness
In *The Structural Transformation of the Public Sphere* (1962), German philosopher and sociologist Jürgen Habermas envisions a protected

space in which private people come together as a public to speak and act in the common interests of the group. Tracing its theoretical origins to the polis of classical Greece, Habermas defines the bourgeois public sphere within the historical, political, and economic parameters of the European Enlightenment. He links its rise to the growth of early capitalism and an emerging communications sector of coffee houses, salons, theaters, literary societies, public libraries, and the daily press. Although this public sphere was also highly exclusionary, it nonetheless opened a space for discussion of social and political life and allowed a reading, self-aware public to critique the policies and activities of the state. Importantly, the public sphere described by Habermas provided a mechanism by which private people were transformed into discursive, active citizens. Despite the importance of mercantilist trade in its early development, the public sphere could not withstand the incursion of advanced capital interests, which co-opted the press in the nineteenth century.

The classical model of the public sphere proposed by Habermas, shored up by a contested history, is rightly subject to critique. A site of privileged, gendered discourse by a reading public with time on its hands, Britain's public sphere was limited to articulate, propertied men of the bourgeoisie. Also problematic are the social and economic differences between the Enlightenment's mercantilism and late capitalism in the twenty-first century. These differences in society, economy, and media notwithstanding, Habermas's public sphere offers a useful paradigm for pursuing public life through discourse—a model of political talk that opens a space for citizen participation.

Other scholars writing in this vein have suggested that an adequate public sphere can be defined by its efforts to construct lively discursive arenas that embrace difference, foster open debate of public issues, and enable purposeful action. Hannah Arendt (1958: 18) noted that powerful public speech actually works to immortalize rhetors, making them part of public memory. In her writings about the early Greeks, she observed that the human condition was seen as a public condition, and to lose one's right to public speech was tantamount to death. Central to her analysis was civic discourse, conducted within a protected public space that promoted participation and shared commitments to the body at large. Dewey (1927: 121) advanced a similar argument by suggesting that a Public emerges only when its members become properly conscious of shared problems—consequences—and take upon themselves the addressing of those problems, each person assuming the appropriate "share according to capacity." He was particularly troubled that the American public of his day seemed "largely inchoate and unorganized," eclipsed, fragmented. For Dewey, an active sphere of public talk was part of the solution. Like Habermas, he viewed communication as the enabler of participatory democracy and the one mechanism by which the public could become aware of deep and common issues uniting its members:

> Without such communication the public will remain shadowy and formless, seeking spasmodically for itself, but seizing and holding its shadow rather than its substance. Till the Great Society is converted into the Great Community, the Public will remain in eclipse. Communication can alone create a great community. Our Babel is not one of tongues but of signs and symbols without which shared experience is impossible. (Dewey 1927: 142)

Certainly not all scholars agree that the Habermasian model holds. Negt and Kluge (1993: 4), for example, posit that the public sphere should be rethought in oppositional terms, as one of women, the working classes, minorities, and other nonelites. Nancy Fraser (1993: 78) demonstrates the gender blindness of Habermas's concept, a critical position also articulated by Cindy Griffin (1996: 23). Both maintain that the traditional public sphere exhibited a masculine bias, privileged elite discourse, and excluded women's voices. Mark Poster (1995: 8), reviewing the configuration of the Internet, claims that the fluidness of cybertexts, the dislocation of speakers, and the spatial character of the Internet itself complicates (and in some cases, renders impossible) the use of this medium in problem-solving conversations. Charles Husband critiques ideal notions of the public sphere, calling the "vision of the media serving as an open conduit for a diverse and contested range of information, opinion and cultural expression" highly improbable (1996: 209). Even so, he argues for a broad, multiethnic form of public talk that positions minority persons and groups as producers and distributors of their own messages. Finally, Jamie Owen Daniel (1997) criticizes the Habermasian model because it admits only "property-owning private people" who know how to speak in public. A partial solution, she suggests, could be found in constituting "public poetry" as a counter–public sphere.

The public sphere of discourse—whether conceptualized as ideal, counter, or multiple—is admittedly elusive. Even so, several ideas emerge as constant threads in formulation of this communication activity. Most scholars of the public sphere suggest that broad access to public, problem-solving speech can lead to increased participation by citizens in the systems and structures that define their lives. A working polis, whose project is engaged public talk, social reform, and a broad-based, popular community, is seen as useful in enabling democracy and a just and fair society. Further, not only is the public sphere conceived as a space in which private individuals become public citizens with commitments to the common, it is also a site in which people become aware of their differences. Characterized by diversity in speech styles, representation, and participation, the public sphere is as much a space for conflict as consensus. Current discussions of the public sphere of discourse rarely cast it as static or monolithic; they focus rather on issues of diversity, tolerance, and alternative lifestyles and experiences. In these analyses, the public sphere becomes a series of fluid and overlapping zones in which a variety of constituencies are granted outlets for public performance in cultural, as well as political, arenas.

However tenuous its connections to current public sphere work, public broadcasting is rooted in progressive notions of public speech, citizenship, and the public good. As chapter 2 delineates, the agenda of the broadcast reform movement included problem-solving public discourse, democratic process, and broad access to media outlets that granted underserved audiences a voice and adequate representation. These possibilities were public sphere possibilities. Although they were narrowed significantly by the successful efforts of commercial broadcasters to restrict spectrum access by noncommercial broadcasters in the 1930s, these precepts are still the work of public broadcasting.

Textual Foundations of Public Service Obligation

Although thousands of pages of public and private discourse have been generated about U.S. noncommercial broadcasting since its inception in the early 1920s, two works in particular surface as important repositories for ideas of public media philosophy and practice. They demonstrate commitment to ideas of a participating and informed public, a culturally diverse public life, and service to underserved audiences. Both were produced by the Carnegie Commission on Educational Television, a nonprofit organization established and funded by the

Carnegie Commission of New York for the express purpose of studying the potential and practical use of noncommercial television in the United States. *Public Television: A Program for Action* was completed in 1967, providing impetus for the Public Broadcasting Act of that year, while *A Public Trust* appeared twelve years later as a critique of the performance of public television.

These reports serve as an index of key terms and concepts developed over time by noncommercial broadcasters about public television's responsibilities to an engaged public life. Although the term "public sphere of discourse" never appears in the commission's findings, public television has from its beginning placed value upon the debate and discussion of public issues. Concerns for an engaged citizenry, a diversity of cultural voices, and a vital public life are seen throughout both documents. The 1967 report opens with an endorsement of the commission's objectives by President Lyndon Johnson, who called on public TV for "enlightenment of our people" and noted that "our freedom depends on the communication of many ideas through many channels" (Carnegie Commission 1967: vii). The report goes on to champion diversity as a staple of American life and public television as its instrument of expression:

> America is geographically diverse, ethnically diverse, widely diverse in its interests. American society has been proud to be open and pluralistic, repeatedly enriched by the tides of immigration and the flow of social thought. Our varying needs and social and intellectual interests are the fabric of the American tradition. (14)

The Carnegie Commission refers to the local community as the heart of public television; admonishes local stations to offer viewers choice and diversity in programming; and urges all local stations to consider their mission as that of a "good metropolitan newspaper," reflecting the entire nation and the world while "maintaining a firm grasp upon the nature and the needs of the people it serves" (87). The commission posits the role of PTV to be one of community involvement and empowerment:

> Public television programming can deepen a sense of community in local life. It can show us our community as it really is. It should be a forum for debate and controversy. It should bring into the home meetings, now generally untelevised, where major public decisions are hammered

out, and occasions where people of the community express their hopes, their protests, their enthusiasms, and their will. It should provide a voice for groups in the community that may otherwise be unheard. (92)

All this is informed by the egalitarian world view of Habermas's ideal public sphere, in which participants meet on equal footing to discuss issues of import to the community. Many times controversial, often a critique of the state and public policy, this kind of public discourse provides not only access to the discussion, but protection from oppression. The authors of *A Program for Action*, like Habermas and Dewey, emphasized the importance of diversity, community, and public talk. They envisioned a media system driven by the needs and goals of the common.

Public TV's failure to follow through on its own vision prompted the second study, in which the Carnegie Commission examined how public television might better achieve its promise. This document explores the rhetoric of public life and diverse community at an even deeper level, and offers a critique of commercial television, marketplace economics, congressional funding practices, and public broadcasting structure. Even with its criticism of the way public television was doing business twelve years after the commission's initial recommendations, *A Public Trust* casts the future and purposes of public television in the democratic frame seen in the first report, citing the system's potential to "inform, engage, enlighten, and delight" and calling the institution of public broadcasting "singularly positioned within the public debate, the creative and journalistic communities, and a technological horizon of uncertain consequences, . . . an absolutely indispensable tool for our people and our democracy" (Carnegie Commission 1979: 12). Public television, the commission reports, can enhance not only "people's lives, but their citizenship as well" within the "diverse cultural and political spectrum" of American social life. Critical to public television's success will be its ability to strike a delicate balance between the system's right to select programming and its responsibilities to a variety of constituent publics: "This balance will yield a public system in which no commercial voice, no single funder voice, no committee voice, no special-interest voice can dominate. A diversity of voices will be heard and many interests may be served (293)." Further, PTV can be an active force in developing authentic community life and the engaged public required to sustain it:

Public broadcasting can easily bring together, face to face, people who might otherwise never meet in daily life. Such communication provides breathtaking potentialities for our sense of community. It can harmonize us in our local concerns. It can bind a nation together by constructing a common catalog of the best in our own society and world culture. A hundred years ago, such experiences were the preserve of a wealthy elite. Now they can be made available to all. (28)

Again, the concepts of the public sphere emerge in this document, which seeks equal access to a modern polis. Participation in the life of the community is extended to all, despite wealth and rank; and the institution of public television, like the institutions of the classical public sphere, facilitates the debate of public problems, goals, and values. In short, although the authors of these two Carnegie Commission reports did not frame their recommendations explicitly within the theoretical context of the public sphere of discourse, their description of public television coheres with the language and expectations theorized by Dewey, Habermas, Arendt, and other scholars of public life. Embedded within these texts is evidence of a sustaining vision of publicness and an institutional world view that values citizen action, critical discussion, multiple voices, and a participatory community life.

An Institution in Crisis

The publicness of the debate notwithstanding, the threat to federal funding in 1996 was only one of the most recent problems confronting public broadcasting—and granting public TV a cushioned and gradual glide path to financial self-sufficiency in no way addresses the core trouble that plagues the system. Even as Big Bird steps off the guillotine, public television sits on the precipice of disaster. While stations compete for limited resources and worry about drops in audience ratings, public TV's institutional identity hangs in the balance. Mired in the struggles of the day-to-day and lacking a clear and precise mission that sets it apart, public broadcasting flounders, and its potential to invigorate public dialogue is slipping away. Given the internal will, public TV could enable the discourses of tolerance, media criticism, and democracy. It could give underserved audiences an outlet for public speech and performance and serve as a springboard for citizen activism. Such public work is threatened, however, by the organization's growing and largely voluntary affiliation with the goals and activities of the market, as seen by the sale of second channel stations, commercialization of its digital spectrum, and enhanced underwriting practices. As public television embraces the commercial model, cashing in on the "PBS brand," viewers increasingly report not being able to discern between public and commercial channels, especially cable offerings such as Arts & Entertainment and Discover. Public TV was clearly established as noncommercial; its increasing privatization is alarming.

So is the lack of commitment by many public TV professionals to the organization's mission of public service. Hoynes interviewed a producer at WGBH/Boston who gave the following assessment of the goals and objectives of public television:

> There are people who take the mission seriously; I know that. I think they are in the minority. . . . There is a sense of knowing that you're working on the best that's being done, and that the films that are being made are serious, and they're films that should be made. . . . That exists, and that's real. Those people are in the minority. (Hoynes 1994: 145)

Another staffer suggested that the lack of vision in public television is due to its institutionalization:

> As anything gets successful it gets more funded and the stakes become higher. And I think what's happened is that public television has become a self-sustaining, self-interested bureaucracy that exists now primarily for its own survival. . . . I don't think people see themselves as missionaries. I don't think people who work in the system see themselves as reformers. (Hoynes 1994: 146)

As the number of public television visionaries declines, either through death or disillusionment, recollections of their aims and purposes dim. Fewer and fewer remember the struggles of public broadcasting's trailblazers; time, silence, and compromises with the market steal their discourses and their passions. This fading of collective memory about public television's original purposes and the genuine fire of its early leaders contributes to the diminishing commitment to public work seen throughout the system.

Just as a failed vision hinders public broadcasting's larger purposes as an agent of participatory democracy, so too does it preclude effective decision making about programming, audience, and economics. A range of operational and funding dilemmas confounds public broadcasters, who face old problems in an increasingly competitive field. Working without a coherent plan rooted in original purposes, public television professionals struggle with diminishing viewership, insufficient resources, and a marginalized stature for public media in the larger culture.

A 1989 study commissioned by the Corporation for Public Broadcasting (CPB) identified a series of systemic problems troubling public television, including a lack of money and infighting at all levels, excessive bureaucracy, rising costs of competing with cable TV, political and financial interference, declining program quality, and a lack of leadership (see "Producers" 1989: 53). Seven years later, a study commissioned by America's Public Television Stations (APTS) produced similar conclusions, reporting that public television is fragmented and lacks internal allegiances; that stations distrust their national organizations, which earn that distrust by fighting among themselves; and that public TV lacks an apparatus for making bold and creative programming decisions (see "PTV" 1996: 17). Day cites the loss of a $5 million grant from the John and Mary Markle Foundation for in-depth and interactive election coverage in 1992 as one among many casualties of the system's inability to act. The Voters' Channel, proposed by Markle Foundation President Lloyd Morrisett, was designed as a counter to the sound bites and photo-ops of typical election reporting. The project was hailed as groundbreaking, but, as Day reports,

> With characteristic caution, PBS stopped short of committing itself to the project and declined to take part in funding the planning phase. . . . By June of 1991, time [had run] out. Morrisett's patience was exhausted; the foot-dragging, the delaying tactics, and PBS's unwillingness to commit itself . . . were too much for even his strong will. He withdrew Markle's offer of the $5 million. "It's very unclear," he noted ruefully, "how they make decisions at PBS." (Day 1995: 3)

The 1996 APTS study also reported that the absence of a system-wide forum for decision making inhibits conflict resolution and splinters the PTV membership. Lacking accepted rules, protocols, and a legitimate sphere for constructive dialogue, public television professionals rarely discuss serious, divisive issues. Instead, said the report, general managers with differing perspectives simply drop out of the national arena due to "pessimism and frustration" ("PTV" 1996: 17).

If station managers drop out, so do viewers. Attracting just 1.7 percent of the nation's TV homes on average during the fourth quarter of 2001, public TV faces the lowest prime-time viewership in its history (Jensen 2002: A1). Increasingly, public television faces a shrinking presence in an ever-widening mix of television programs, threatened especially by aggressive cable networks that woo—and win—PTV audiences. Once the sole source for the "safely splendid," as well as a Friday night public affairs strip, PBS now competes with the Disney, Discovery, Arts & Entertainment, American Movie Classics, Bravo, and C-Span channels for the arts and public affairs audience once considered public TV's core constituency. Even American children, once considered part and parcel of the PTV audience, now look not only to public television but also to commercial sources—taping their favorite shows, renting videos, and even viewing established PBS favorites on cable TV. Prime examples are *Magic School Bus*, *Shining Time Station*, and *Mumfie*, which headlined the fall lineup for Fox Kids Network in 1998. Public TV programmers are rightly worried that their stations will lose audience for their afternoon and Saturday morning kids' blocks as children move to commercial channels. Meeting with station programmers in February 2002, PBS president and CEO Pat Mitchell warned that PBS's disconnect with American viewers may cost the system its future:

> Not only are we not top of mind, we are dangerously close in our overall prime-time number to falling below the relevance quotient. And if that happens, we will surely fall below any arguable need for government support, not to mention corporate or individual support. There is a level beyond which we cannot go and still claim to be a universal service. (qtd. in Jensen 2002: A1)

The system's growing dependence on private sector funding has also pushed it to gear programming to the tastes of upscale viewer-donors and corporate underwriters. The result, as Hoynes reports, is class-based "quality TV":

> "Quality television" is the kind of programming that appeals to highly educated people. It differs from commercial television not because there is no concern for audience but rather because it appeals to a different, more select audience. Essentially, the term "quality television" has become a code for elitist, highbrow programs. Such quality programs are, not coincidentally, also the kinds of programs that are perceived to be "safe"—they contain a minimum amount of controversy and they appeal to corporate funders, well-off members of the public, and prestigious critics. These kinds of quality programs serve the interests and reflect the tastes of important people within the public television orbit. At the same time, they clearly differentiate public television from commercial television—largely along class lines. (1994: 154)

Just as public television offers up a safe and marketable "quality text" to individual and corporate donors, its underwriting guidelines limit minority representation by prohibiting the financial support of "interested" social and political groups. For example, Charles Guggenheim's thoughtful documentary about the civil rights movement, "A Time for Justice," did not air on public television because production funding had been provided by the Southern Poverty Law Center (Guggenheim 1996). Similarly, "Out of Work," a documentary about two gay men and a lesbian who were fired after coworkers learned they were gay, was rejected because its funders included nine labor unions and the Astraea National Lesbian Action Foundation. PBS explained that the underwriters–"all sort of labor related"—could create a perception of conflict of interest (Ledbetter 1997: 6). Analysts have pointed critically to the many PBS series and documentaries funded by corporate entities having "interest" in the content of the programs. Examples include *ExxonMobil Masterpiece Theatre* and *Wall Street Week With Fortune* (which actually promote sponsors in their program titles), as well as *Antiques Roadshow,* a popular series funded by a firm that insures antiques and collectibles (Newman 2001: B1). Corporate interest permeates these funding relationships.

Even more problematic, however, is the structure of exclusion that frames the conflict-of-interest rule for social and political groups. The constituencies they represent frequently inhabit the margins of social life; they lack not only political and economic power but also access to "appropriate" funders. How else to hear the voices of these people and grant them rights to public deliberation, but through the resources of groups close to them? Public television's timidity, lack of commitment to marginal groups, and reluctance to acknowledge that every text is shaped by its producer's interests speaks to the system's unwillingness to represent the whole of the nation.

Lashley (1992b: 95) argues that PBS's treatment of ethnic minorities is especially limited. She claims that of 9,202 programs aired by public television stations in 1986, 75.5 percent featured no racial or ethnic minorities. Of those programs that included minority content, 71 percent were aimed at children, 28.8 percent were for adult viewers, and the balance (.2 percent) were intended for teens. This meager representation of minority experience can be attributed to small numbers of minority managers and producers in public TV, as well as the system's practice of developing programming for an ideal donor-type seen generally as white, middle-class, and professional. According to Lashley (1992b: 103), demographic analyses of public television membership have identified subscribers largely as nonblack, college-educated, higher-income, and highly skilled. Not only are these viewers perceived as individuals capable of making several donations each year, they are also the audiences sought by corporate marketing executives as consumers for their goods and services. In light of these financial goals, minority programming is often deliberately excluded from fundraising efforts because development officers claim, many times unfairly, that minority donors give less often, make smaller pledges, and have lower fulfillment and additional gift rates. Those stations seeking minority programs for their fundraising and general program schedules are hard pressed to find them. Despite the sprinkling of ethnic faces in kids' shows such as *Sesame Street* and *Zoom*, very few programs are being produced for Hispanics, Asians, and African Americans. Even a perusal of PBS library services offers but a handful. In 1988, Sen. Daniel Inouye (D-Hawaii) observed that "blacks and Hispanics alone constitute 30 percent of our nation's population. The need for programming addressing these audiences, including foreign language programming, should be a primary concern of public radio and television stations and the CPB" (qtd. in Lashley 1992b: 64). Fifteen years later, whether during prime time, fringe, or pledge week, programs produced by and for audiences at the margin remain uncommon on public television. *American Family*, premiering in January 2002 and celebrated by CPB as the first Latino drama series to air on U.S. television, is admittedly a positive step. Even so, its late entrance onto the American social scene, coupled with the fact that it was originally conceived for CBS, is evidence of public broadcasting's failed leadership in developing substantive programming for ethnic groups in this country. Public stations could well look to Telemundo affiliate KVDA/San Antonio for innovative programming ideas. This local station, seeking to reestablish a connection with viewers alienated by news programs, has placed news cameras in the neighborhood and granted local citizens the right to report their own news. KVDA expects to equip as many as thirty households with technology to provide a neighborhood slant on events that would go unnoticed otherwise (Huesca 2001: B8). These experiments in news gathering, rightly the domain of public media, are virtually unknown in public television.

Just as public television tends to ignore audiences at the edges, it marginalizes voices exploring controversial perspectives through independent documentary film. Independent producer B. J. Bullert (1995: xvii) reports that her labor movement documentary, "Earl Robinson: Ballad of an American," was rejected by PBS national programmers in 1994. Like other documentary producers dealing with topics lying outside an established American consensus, her experiences with managers and programmers of PBS stations have proved contentious. PBS policies, as well as public television's general worries about public controversy, have worked to contain the critical, outsider viewpoints of individual producers and the independent filmmaker community in general. The demand by PBS programming for objectivity and balance, its concern about any piece with a point of view, and a complete disdain for advocacy journalism preclude many works by producers who use film as an instrument for social change. The "editorial" film, with its passionate, often personal and political statement, is shoved to the periphery of the PBS schedule, if indeed it is aired at all. Describing the machinations of PBS in denying "Dark Circle," a documentary about the nuclear power industry, a slot in the schedule in 1986, Bullert quotes PBS programmer Gail Christian, who was alone in supporting broadcast of the now-acclaimed film: "Once again public television [looked] like a bunch of fools. The [review] panel was six little quakey, shaky people in a room" (1995: 49).

PBS has since developed a limited venue for point-of-view programs in *P.O.V.*, a series that typically airs once a week in late prime or fringe time. Even so, the independent film, and the producer and constituent voices it represents, is still an anomaly on public television. Its presence in the national schedule has been jeopardized by too little commitment to television as a change agent, a systemwide nervousness about controversial texts, and unstable funding mechanisms for independent film production. Only a last-minute Senate committee move in April 1996 saved the budget of the Independent Television Service (ITVS), which CPB president Richard Carlson argued was wasteful spending ("Carlson Sees Waste" 1996: 8). ITVS, which was developed by Congress to increase the diversity of programs on public TV, stands by the motto "public television for a change" (Bullert 1995: 198; Daressa 1996: 20). It is a rare source of television programs dedicated to preserving and enlarging the public sphere.

Finally, adequate funding for public media has been problematic since noncommercial broadcasting went on the air in the 1920s. The system's financial straits derive fundamentally from the early and internationally unprecedented decision by the United States to allow market forces to control development of all American broadcasting. After attending the 1931 World Conference on Radio in Vienna and examining the broadcasting systems of twenty-nine countries, Armstrong Perry, representing the National Committee on Education by Radio, observed that U.S. commitments to capitalist media were unique:

> The information gathered indicated that the United States stands alone among the nations of the world in its policy of placing radio channels in the hands of commercial concerns to be used as they see fit. . . . Advertisers are permitted to buy time in some countries, but they do not dominate the air. (qtd. in Blakely 1979: 27)

Despite public sympathies for noncommercial radio and a vigorous (though disorganized) broadcast reform effort, by the mid-1930s U.S. broadcasting had become a for-profit, advertising-supported medium. Protected funding and set-aside spectrum for public media were largely nonexistent until FM channels were allocated for educational radio in the mid-forties and very limited federal funding was initiated for public television in the late sixties. In both cases, the support was too little and too late. Over the last seventy years, public broadcasting has struggled to overcome this early, and structuring, debility that forces it to go before Congress, hat in hand, every three years for operational funds, and to appeal to viewers at least four times a year in comprehensive on-air, telemarketing, and direct mail fundraising campaigns. Even with annual auctions and corporate support, the results barely cover the bills; too little is left over for innovative, televisual incursions into public life.

Although there was a call for adequate public funding when the Public Broadcasting Act was passed in 1967, the Carnegie Commission's recommendation of a receiver excise tax did not pass congressional muster, and Lyndon Johnson's reported intent to build a funding structure for the system never materialized (Hoynes 1994: 3, 22). Since 1968—when Congress authorized $9 million for public broadcasting, but appropriated no monies at all—PTV has not only been strapped for funds, but dependent upon the largesse of a less-than-generous U.S. Congress that has yet to establish a long-term and protected funding base (PBS 1996a: 1). This financial insecurity has at times teetered precariously on extinguishment of all public resources, as when Richard Nixon vetoed a three-year appropriation in 1972 and sent the word that he wanted public TV out of the public affairs business. Although a scaled-down version of the funding bill eventually passed, it did so only after significant compromise that tied federal funding to matching grants from the private sector. The 1972 veto also led to a reconfigured CPB board of directors that put conservatives intent on "correcting" the "left leaning" tilt of public affairs programs at the helm. *Bill Moyers' Journal* and *Washington Week in Review* were among programs the new CPB board did not fund (Bullert 1995: 17–19). Within ten years, the system would be under attack again, as the Reagan administration called for the total defunding of public television in 1981. Barry Chase, vice president of news and public affairs programming at PBS during the 1980s, remembers the political climate of his tenure as repressive: "There was a widespread fear that if the system were too troublesome, it could be shut down completely" (qtd. in Bullert 1995: 19).

The most recent large-scale political threat to public television came in 1995–96, with legislation before the 104th Congress. Had the deep budget cuts proposed early in the session by key House Republicans been enacted, no station in the system would have been untouched. All would have been forced to cancel programs, curtail projects, and release staff. Some—especially small, rural operations—would surely have faced closure. Supporters of public media, including APTS lobbyists, staff of public TV and public radio stations, legislators, and members of the public, rallied to prevent initial cuts of $100 million for 1995 and zero-based funding over a three-year period. In addition, their efforts restored $25 million to the 1999 appropriation and froze funding at $250 million through 2000. The Public Telecommunications Facilities Program, cut by a third and funded out of the House Appropriations Committee at $10.25 million for FY 1997, was returned to its 1996 funding level of $15.25 million. Three Education Department television projects focusing on early childhood learning and literacy maintained level funding for 1996: Star Schools received $30 million, Ready to Learn was funded at $7 million, and Mathline kept its allocation of slightly over $1 million dollars (PBS 1996b: 1).

As critical as these measures were in shoring up the short-term survival of public TV, the pre-Gingrich annual budget for public broadcasting, only half the cost of one B-2 bomber, represented a tiny fraction of total federal spending (Nelson 1995: 16). The per capita tax expenditure of just over one dollar for U.S. public broadcasting, likened by Vice President Al Gore to the cost of two candy bars, pales in comparison with the federal allocations of other countries (Edwards 1995c: C1). The per capita cost for public broadcasting in the United Kingdom is $38.56. In Canada, it is $32.15. In Japan, $17.71 (Shales 1995: B1). The absence of public funding at a comparable level for U.S. public broadcasting is a shrill and poignant testament to public television's failure to compel a passionate defense by the nation.

American radio's laissez-faire origins resonate in contemporary funding debates for public broadcasting. This long-standing tradition of marketplace media economics cannot be discounted in assessing public broadcasting's internal and external problems. Even so, the system's inability to sustain a financial and cultural foothold in American social life is symptomatic of a deep-seated and destructive failure of confidence by public broadcasters. Although public television has the potential to enlarge and invigorate the lives of all Americans, the average viewing household tunes in for less than eight hours each month. One American in ten who watches, gives (PBS 1996c: 1). Without commitments and practices that make it invaluable to the American public, public TV can be seen only as a luxury, an add-on, peripheral to the lives of the citizenry. Defined as an alternative to mainstream broadcasting, PTV sits on the margins, comfortably outside the fray of a noisy, conflicted public life. The costs of such political comfort are dear. That the U.S. Congress has consistently refused to build a protected funding base for public media; that the public does not actually demand adequate support for PTV; and that its supporters frame their arguments in metaphors of children's programs speak to public broadcasting's lack of centrality in American lives.

This is not to say that public television's efforts have been entirely unsuccessful. They have not. Indeed, even when facing changes in audience behaviors, as well as its own problems of funding, internal structure, and program selection, the system has moved clumsily, autonomously forward. PTV has sought to serve local programming needs while broadcasting a national schedule; to provide programs for use in public schools while not being overly "educational" during prime time; and to produce and air programs of interest and use to a range of publics while still attracting local and national underwriting support. There have been moments of extraordinary service, many of them in technological innovation: the first hour-long national newscast, closed captioning for the hearing impaired, interactive television, satellite program distribution, and FM simulcast of live musical events. Even so, what emerges is a system in crisis, a slow, meandering, drifting crisis that is leading public television to an acceptance of the "glide path."

The Call for Vision: A Decades-Old Critique

Diminished audiences and revenues, faltering identity, battles inside and out, and an acknowledged lack of leadership have persuaded some public broadcasters to move even further within the mainstream of capitalist media. Seeking direction from the marketplace, they have chosen to mime commercial broadcasting's goals of higher ratings, hit series, and programming appealing to individual donors and corporate underwriters.

Others insist that public broadcasting's survival depends upon a clearly articulated and system-wide mission of public service. This call for vision is not new. For years, critics—many of them public broadcasters—have claimed the system operates without a sure sense of purpose or identity. Returning to his office at the Rockefeller Foundation following the Allerton House meetings of 1949, John Marshall bemoaned the narrow perspective of the educational broadcasters. Writing in his personal desk diary for August 11, 1949, Marshall noted:

> In general the response to all this was somewhat disappointing. [Charles] Siepmann volunteered the opinion that little could be ex-pected from this particular group. [Thomas] Baird's view of them is that they are incredibly timid without prestige in their own institutions and apparently unaware of what they could do if they were to recognize their real freedom to act. (Rockefeller Foundation Papers)

Former PBS president Larry Grossman echoed these frustrations in 1987, when he called public broadcasting a system at war with itself, with practices that kept it trapped in "second-class status, . . . a hand-icap in attracting or retaining truly creative and talented people, and an incapacity to make timely program decisions" (qtd. in Sucherman 1987: 68). Day, a former chief executive of WNET/New York, made similar charges as he grieved a lost vision and said public television was "an institution of enormous promise mired in a self-created bureau-cracy" (1995: 4). In June 1996, forty-six years after the agenda-setting of the Allerton House Seminar, the system's National Program Policy Committee was still calling on PBS to develop a programming mission: "What is urgently needed . . . is the articulation of a vision and plan for the NPS (National Program Service) in meaningful dialogue with the system. The NPS must regularly provide access to a multiplicity of voices, views, and perspectives . . . to be relevant to the population" (qtd. in Bedford 1996: 1). Like other advocates (and critics) of public broadcasting, these leaders from within the system have sought ways for public media to achieve its potential as a visionary and disciplined provider of quality service. All perceive a coherent public mission as central to that goal.

The consequences of operating without a commonly understood purpose are grave. Not only does the absence of an underpinning mis-sion preclude effective resource management, it also hinders stable funding, creative service for the nation's publics, and a unifying desire for social change. After analyzing public television's workplace dy-namics, BMR Associates described a fragmented organization without a clear sense of its future or its past:

> Our present hypothesis is that, as time has passed, the sense of national mission and purpose has slowly eroded. . . . There is neither a unifying

vision nor a set of stabilizing forces to unify PTV. Internally, there is no clear over-arching vision around which the various perspectives can rally. There is no unifying voice, nor is there even agreement on whether there should be such a voice. ("PTV" 1996: 17)

As a result, said the consultants, local licensees feel less responsibility for the welfare of other stations and the national institution itself, revealing a startling instability in the organization's foundation. This report resonates with the critique offered up twenty years ago by Ray Hurlbert, a founder of Alabama ETV. Hurlbert's 1981 oral history interview with James Robertson charged that public television historically has lacked a sense of national cohesion:

[Public TV] is a team of horses with no reins or no bridles or no connection, just . . . 18 or 20 or 50 horses with no controls, and you have all kinds of prima-donnas and private interests and independent insurgents almost, you might say, to where it has made the control disruptive. . . . We don't have any semblance of unity. (Hurlbert 1981)

The direct result, said Hurlbert, was a radical reduction in federal funding in the early 1980s:

The reason that the appropriations [were] cut for public television was that they did not feel that it was imperative or essential or necessary. Now when any government or any institution finds out that something is absolutely necessary, they're going to have it. But they found out that we hadn't any unity . . . or any cooperation in our organization, and they said that we were ineffective and we hadn't been doing what we set out to do. We were actually chasing rabbits. (20)

Finally, Williard Rowland maintains that complacency and a dangerous ease with the status quo are the most debilitating effects of operating without a powerful vision:

U.S. public broadcasting is nowhere near as significant a force as it ought to be and yet, internally, it is remarkably quiescent on that score. . . . [It] can do much more by way of vital programming, information and educational services that simply will not exist in American life without it. . . . But it cannot do these things if the institution itself has no internal gyroscope—no vision of what is possible, no burning fire in the belly, and no willingness to challenge the stultifying forces that surround and seduce it. (1993: 190)

Hoynes (1994: 138) and Lashley (1992b: 45) have both suggested that public television's organizational behavior is structured largely for survival. Following their reasoning, the absence of a clearly stated vision may actually work to public television's advantage in the short term by making the organization less accountable to public scrutiny. If the system occupies a small corner of the mass media environment and does not attract attention as the carrier of a strong service ethos, it may not be targeted simply because its goals are less well known and its performance cannot be easily evaluated. In the long term, however, such a strategy can be life-threatening, as it costs public TV its collective identity and a hope for the future. "Without an identity," writes Hoynes, "it is virtually impossible to envision the future, let alone formulate and articulate a mission" (149). Even so, some public television professionals are content to operate without a mission. They suggest that common visions necessarily invoke centralized bureaucracy, at significant cost to station autonomy and its effective participation in the local community. It is ironic that notions of localism have been called upon to undermine ideas of a systemwide agenda of social practice. Legitimately a part of public broadcasting's philosophical heritage and consistent with Dewey's emphasis on the power of face-to-face communication in maintaining responsive and participatory democracy, concerns for the local have generated some of public television's finest moments in helping communities address their problems. Writing twenty-four years ago, Stephen White, assistant to the chairman of the Carnegie Commission, called the debate of local versus national "a strawman and . . . never anything else. . . . The system absolutely requires both" (qtd. in Blakely 1979: 205). Yet fueled by fear of lost revenues, redirected power, and oppressive and centralized bureaucratic control, many station managers continue to use appeals to localism in resisting ideas that might unify public television within a shared, collectively determined purpose (Ryan 1997).

Certainly, the PTV situation is complicated. Public television is an underfunded, nonprofit broadcasting system operating in a capitalist market economy. It developed within a liberal-pluralist environment that advocated an evolving, organic practice for institutional definition. Direct interference by government and other powerful agencies was to be avoided at all costs, and the system was expected, over time, to accommodate to, and thrive within, the American political economy. That it has survived—and survived well enough to broadcast a full day's schedule to almost every household in America—is no small feat. Even so, lying below the surface are deeper questions of institutional selfhood. What is the system's responsibility in addressing national and global social problems? Who should constitute the PTV audience? How can public TV offer a forum for differing ideological, cultural, and political discourses? And finally, what does it really mean to be "public"?

Without its own unique identity, public TV will continue to flounder in an increasingly complicated media environment of satellites, cable, pay-for-view, niche programming, and the prospect of 500 digital channels. Lacking a common direction, a usable past, and a believable future, public television is hard pressed to compete for financial resources or an audience base. This hinders its ability to produce compelling programs, to serve diverse communities, and to initiate a conversation about national values. Importantly, without a public vision, public television cannot fill up the vast wasteland that American television remains.

The history of public broadcasting is a slippery and complicated tale of intellectual currents, political battles, layered discourse, and vested interests at every turn. It is a history framed by questions of genre, funding, production control; worries over partisanship, radical voices, and the role of social critique; celebration of quality, education, and high culture. It involves notions of active citizenship, access to a public forum, and community. Traces of its discourse permeate our cultural forms. This book seeks to access and analyze this complicated social institution by reclaiming the central arguments of its collective vision, recovering the details of its progressive struggle for resources, and fleshing out the complex discourses surrounding three important moments of its past.

These historical moments—one during the Great Depression, one during the Cold War, and one during the social protests of the 1960s— engaged a national audience in efforts to further the structural and philosophic interests of public broadcasting in America. Although decades apart and situated in different social and political environments, each involved an important fight for resources, encapsulated noncommercial broadcasting's central arguments, and engendered formal action that moved public media from a world of ideas into one of policy, regulation, spectrum allocation, and capital. In these three events, the dominant discourse of public media advocates coalesced around ideas of a participatory public, cultural diversity, vigorous public discussion, and citizen access to governance. As Ralph Engelman (1996: 13) suggests, these definitions of public media stem from early public notions of American broadcasting, which viewed the airwaves as a public resource and a tool for democracy. The PTV mission is also rooted in the traditions of American progressivism and its commitments to participatory democracy, social reform, and socially responsible public speech. The words and deeds of public broadcasters resonate with Dewey's belief in the common good, that "one day we as a society can become one people, . . . and we can legitimately speak of collective social progress" (qtd. in Campbell 1992: 47). However, the conversation about noncommercial broadcasting has never been simple, monolithic, or even consistent. Indeed, Wagner-Hatfield, the FCC spectrum allocations, and the Public Broadcasting Act were not only important fights for facilities; each also served as a locus of debate for conflicting visions about noncommercial media, and each hinted at the failed resolve that has prevented public media's full development as an agent of the public sphere. The account is complicated, a story of ambiguity and colliding points of view.

It is also a tale of tragedy. Early radio in the United States was a diverse and talkative medium. Until the mid-1920s noncommercial interests controlled almost a third of the band, offering space on the dial to a range of constituencies, including religious groups, civic organizations, labor, arts groups, socialists, farmers, and educators. Over the years these voices dwindled, leaving a public broadcasting system that has privileged the mainstream discourses of elites and education. The audible silences of labor, religion, agriculture, and the left speak to public television's failure to enable a cohesive and diverse community sustained by performative public speech. The mission of public broadcasting has been jeopardized by the system's compromises, its lack of dedication to social change, and at times an outright indifference to an invisible public.

The historical recovery (and critique) of institutional purpose for public media seems an important contribution to offer in the early twenty-first century, as the debate over communication industry policy is increasingly framed in terms of the global market, and American public television—like public service broadcasting systems in England, Holland, Germany, Italy, Canada, Denmark, and France—faces a crisis of funding and institutional identity (Avery 1993: xvii). Indeed, the threat of reductions in federal funding in the mid-1990s set in motion, however quietly, the dismantling of part of the U.S. public television structure. WNYC-TV, a public service TV station operating on a commercial license in New York City, was sold in June 1996, so its board could continue operations of two city-owned public radio stations, WNYC-FM and WNYC-AM. Alternative in format and content, WNYC-TV resembled a coalition of turn-of-the-century foreign-language newspapers, broadcasting to the city's "forgotten communities" of teens, gays, and non–English speakers, among others. The city, said management, couldn't afford to keep all three; it sacrificed one public station to save two (Blumenthal 1995: C14).

The events of 1934 and 1950–51 were points of rupture in a narrative dominated by for-profit broadcasting in this country. In each case, the possibility of the moment was contained largely by the action of the FCC, which preserved the market-driven status quo by denying noncommercial broadcasters access to the radio spectrum: recommending against set-aside frequencies for noncommercial radio in 1934 and allocating most of the usable TV band to commercial broadcasters in 1950–51. The result was fewer stations in the hands of people representing public interests. The traditional constituencies of public media—labor, education, agriculture, civic and arts groups, and religious organizations—were frozen out in favor of capitalists.

Today, ironically, the function of containing public broadcasting's public mission has been assumed by the Corporation for Public Broadcasting and public broadcasting professionals who embrace free market rules and rewards. Developed as a political insulator for public television and public radio, CPB in recent years has become a conductor for a conservative ideology bent on privatization of public institutions. One policy shift in the allocation of federal monies, in particular, reflects the aggressive move of free market mores into the corporate culture of public broadcasting. CPB announced in July 1996 that it would cut back funding for multistation markets, providing a single base grant in each of these markets to be split among grantees. As a result, Maine Public Broadcasting closed the second channel it created in a 1993 consolidation, and WQED-TV's board of directors announced intentions to sell WQEX, its alternative-programming sister in Pittsburgh. As this policy continues, other stations will be silenced or altered.

More than forty communities, including San Francisco, Los Angeles, Seattle, Denver, Chicago, and Atlanta, currently support two or more public stations, and data suggest that 60 percent of the American population receives more than one PTV channel. The 1996 funding guidelines urge these stations to respond "collaboratively" to the allo-cation of a single grant. In reality, say public broadcasters, larger sta-tions will prevail, and smaller operations will either go black or de-velop a new, market-oriented funding base (Behrens 1996b: 1).

Although Thomas McCourt (1996: 24) reports little redundancy in public television program schedules, there is in fact much duplication of programs and programming type among overlap stations. Even with a valid critique of PTV program duplication, however, discontinuing funds for overlapping service is a serious detriment to public media pur-pose in this country. Not only does this regulatory practice support a sin-gle mainstream schedule for all PBS stations, it also acts against localism, cultural diversity, and minority interest. Importantly, by reducing the number of stations available to serve a range of publics, this CPB rule also precludes the possibility for reform. The ideas of communication theorist James Curran and independent producer Lawrence Daressa could both usefully inform an innovative reconfiguration of public elec-tronic space. Curran (1996: 57) argues for a multistation structure, and Daressa suggests that "public TV should be heterogeneous, even contra-dictory . . . deliberately mixing points of view and artistic approaches . . . inviting the discontinuities, the ruptures of democratic debate" (1990). Without spectrum assets, however, proponents of such reform are effectively locked outside the gate of public media practice.

Public media old-timers (who remember the bitter fights for spectrum space) and public media historians (who record them) count the "one grant per market" rule as a grave threat to the system. As Terrel Cass, president of WLIW, an overlap public TV station in Long Island, noted in 1996: "We need *more* shelf space in public television, not less. We have hundreds of commercial channels with garbage. If we can't have two or three places with quality television, what's our society coming to?" (qtd. in Behrens 1996a: 11). Clearly, in developing funding policies for over-lapping stations, CPB's objective has been to reduce public broadcasting's duplicative infrastructure, not to encourage the use of that infrastructure for diverse services. Critics inside the system and out have argued that CPB should support structures and activities that provide strong local ac-cess and control: not only funding stations with differentiated program-ming, but exploring strategies that broaden alternative service. The de-velopment of such policies seems remote, however, as public broadcasting moves increasingly to mirror for-profit models of standardization and con-solidation. Five years after Cass's impassioned plea for "more shelf space,"

WLIW/21 announced its merger with WNET/13, the country's largest public television station. Despite public criticism and the resignation of one of its board members, WLIW voted to transfer all its assets to Channel 13 in exchange for WNET's support in digital conversion (Ramos 2001: A7). The choice was driven largely by economics. As Cass reported in 2001, "We're under a lot of pressure, with the federal funds we do get, that we become more efficient" (qtd. in Huff 2001: 67).

This merger of the largest and fourth largest public stations in the country will create a megastation not unlike other conglomerates in U.S. media. Although touted by some as a successful effort toward CPB's goal of "creative collaborative infrastructure," this merger stands as evidence of a failed public mission, further marginalizing the needs and interests of neighborhood constituents. Further, to advocate this model as a strategic prototype for other overlapping stations facing a similar shortfall in CPB funding seems not only shortsighted but grossly irresponsible. Public television's foundations place the system's commitments clearly in broad public service; the CPB overlapping market policies provide little to no protection for old visions or new opportunities. Rather, the Corporation's "one-per-market" rule acts to reduce stations, centralize public media programming, and blunt minority speech. The glide path to self-sufficiency, which forces stations to scramble and sacrifice for increasingly scarce resources, takes few survivors at the margin. Without a clearly articulated statement of organizational mission, public broadcasters lack the creative resources to fight these trends.

In *All That Is Solid Melts Into Air*, Marshall Berman recalls Pushkin's horrifying tale of Evgeny, a young Russian clerk pursued night after night through the streets of St. Petersburg by the animated statue of Peter the Great. Mounted on a rearing copper steed, the Bronze Horseman finally chases Evgeny out of his mind and away from the city. Still, the "copper Horseman comes behind, his charger's gallop ringing brass; and all night long, turn where Evgeny will, the Copper Horseman's clattering hoofbeats hammer." In the spring, Evgeny's body is washed ashore, "and there for charity's sake they buried his cold corpse." His final words of despair—"You'll reckon with me yet!"—proved hopeless. Flung in terror, defiance, even rebellion, these words rang against the cobblestones of a silent, private space in the backstreets of St. Petersburg. Berman suggests safety from state oppression was to be found in the Nevsky Prospect, a boulevard of light and gaslight, foreign goods, artisan shops, and nobles' palaces. A free and cosmopolitan zone, the Nevsky was "the one public place where all Petersburgers could present themselves and interact with one another without having to look behind and listen for the Bronze Horseman's hooves" (Berman 1982: 80). As Americans living in the twenty-first century, we are not Pushkin's Evgeny, pursued by a statue of Peter the Great. Even so, we are not without our own Bronze Horsemen: worries about personal safety and national security, the threat of global warming, and children living in East St. Louis who cannot now and may never learn to read. Modern life has brought isolation, alienation, and a rationalizing political economy that offers too little time and space of the "in-between" for creative process and work. And in it all, we long to put personal and public lives together.

Public television could become America's Nevsky Prospect. Boldly reconceived and appropriately funded, this seventy-five-year-old media institution has potential to be a public space for free and open discourse about what ails our society—binding Americans together as a participatory public; offering up a protected zone for performative, political talk; and inspiring a rich, collective life. There is much at risk for public broadcasting and the American people it would serve, and despite the well-intentioned gestures of Congresswoman Lowey, the stakes stretch beyond the metaphors of children's television. This is a battle over how public media resources are to be used in building effective, optimistic communities in the coming century, and our national identity as a people of talk and action capable of solving social problems hangs in the balance. In a world of unexpected pregnancies, racial tensions, schools that don't reach the kids they aim to teach, outright poverty, and families that fall apart, Sesame Street's giant yellow canary needs all the help he can get. Without the support of a powerfully diverse and committed public life, Big Bird can hardly withstand the hooves of the Horseman.

CHAPTER TWO

A Stewardship of Compromise: Public Television and the Radio Spectrum

On January 21, 1935, the Federal Communications Commission announced its decision to deny a spectrum set-aside for nonprofit radio. The Wagner-Hatfield Amendment, language that could have altered the course of American broadcasting, was officially dead, as was the broadcast reform movement of the 1920s and 1930s. Nonprofit radio, born in a moment of multivocal diversity and fueled by talk of publicness and community, found itself on the street, without a funding base or even a place on the dial.

This relegation of noncommercial radio to the margins of American broadcasting was not achieved overnight or without a fight. The margin of the Senate vote that decided Wagner-Hatfield on May 15, 1934—forty-two nays and twenty-three ayes—and the unanimous FCC decision six months later should not be taken as evidence that the fight for broadcast reform was easily conceded, that it lacked an impassioned campaign, or that the historical moment was without possibility. Indeed, the vigor of the reform movement and its leaders' ties to mainstream philosophic traditions privileging public speech and participation, the state of social and political fluidity that characterized the Depression years, especially 1933 and 1934, and the rise of progressive ideas that saw passage of a range of New Deal set-aside legislation all point to a moment in American history when broadcast reform legislation could have been enacted, ultimately changing the practice of American broadcasting in profound ways.

The social, historical moment that provided a forum for discourse about radio, democracy, and culture, opening windows of possibility for nonprofit broadcasting, was also a political moment in which the discourse of social democracy ran headlong into the practice of capitalism. For the proponents of commercial broadcasting, what was at stake was not free speech, publicness, literacy, and notions of community, but rather resources, radio frequencies that offered up access to a new market. For this reason, nonprofit radio could not be allowed to win; and while nonprofit broadcasters waged their battle for reform largely in public, calling upon the efficacy of their ideas and purposes, commercial broadcasters fought in private, working to control key committee votes that could open the spectrum to nonprofit ownership. This historical moment, filled with the promises of social change, was also grounded in a political reality controlled by men determined to keep nonprofit radio off the air.

Section 307(c) came before the American public and the Federal Communications Commission in the autumn of 1934. The last public battle for control of the U.S. airwaves until the FCC allocations of TV frequencies in 1952, this amendment to the Communications Act of 1934 called for a study into the set-aside of radio channels for nonprofit radio. The broadcast reform movement would fail, and miserably, before the tightly orchestrated and lavishly financed opposition of commercial broadcasters. Even so, the concepts underpinning nonprofit radio were not inappropriate to the historical moment; and the possibilities for media reform were significant. Had the set-aside been approved and early stations granted adequate means for funding, American broadcasting could conceivably have seen a more decentralized structure of ownership and control, greater diversity of programs, service to minority audiences, and a diminished collusion in mainstream consumer culture with advertising. Even though they were defeated, the Wagner-Hatfield Amendment and Section 307(c) were nonetheless pivotal in efforts by noncommercial broadcasters to establish a space for public media in U.S. culture. Not only did they engender a widespread public debate about mass media structure and policy, they worked to establish a philosophic and strategic foundation for noncommercial television's successful bid for reserved frequencies in 1950–51.

Clearly, the 1920s and 1930s were critical moments in the development of U.S. broadcasting. This period of media history witnessed the birth of radio and its rapid development in the United States, from one facility in 1920 to 733 in 1927. These were years that established not only parameters of regulation and genre, but also central definitions of practice and identity. Patterns, policies, and ideas about institutional culture, for both commercial and noncommercial broadcasting, were products of this seminal moment. Importantly, it was during this period, after a prolonged battle over spectrum allocation and control, that U.S. broadcasting evolved into the for-profit, advertising-driven enterprise that defines American electronic media today. This chapter examines an important moment in this media history, the 1934 FCC study into a spectrum set-aside for noncommercial radio, and focuses on choices and discourse that worked to anchor commercial and noncommercial broadcasting to the same narrative of network dominance. Just as Section 307(c) provided noncommercial broadcasters a small and contested space of possibility, it also demonstrated the reformers' lack of coherence as a group and their failed commitments to popular ownership of the airwaves. The compromises of public media, seen over the years in public broadcasters' choices to privilege instructional programs during the day and elite culture at night, had their beginnings in the spectrum debates of 1934.

This analysis of noncommercial broadcasters' discourse about protected spectrum focuses on that of their opponents—specifically, the campaign developed by public relations practitioner Ivy Ledbetter Lee for Columbia Broadcasting System (CBS) and the hearings statement he drafted for CBS president William S. Paley. Lee employed strategies that reframed the rhetorical environment. He also appropriated the arguments and central identity of his opponents and reversed and redefined key terms of the debate. Accurately assessing broad public support for the tenets of nonprofit radio, Lee encapsulated and co-opted those precepts in naming the qualities of his client. Casting CBS as the white knight of radio programming, Lee also defined noncommercial broadcasters as fractious, inept, and undeserving of the "desirable wave lengths." The result was a persuasive campaign that worked to maintain corporate ownership of the airwaves in the mid-thirties and to solidify long-term policy defining the spectrum as a resource for commercial broadcasting.

Especially pertinent is a five-page memorandum written by Lee for the final stages of the CBS campaign against the nonprofit spectrum set-aside. Drafted in September 1934, after the defeat of the Wagner-Hatfield Amendment in May and the passage into law two months later of the Communications Act of 1934, this document regarding Columbia's presentation to the FCC is admittedly a small part of the 14,000 pages of text produced during those hearings. Nonetheless, it fleshes out the discourse of an important event in U.S. broadcasting history, detailing the persuasive elements of a little-known corporate public relations campaign that had long-lasting policy effects, and demonstrating specific ways in which corporate advocacy has been structured to advance broadcasting regulation and policy. Importantly, the memo also exemplifies insider discourse for both commercial and noncommercial broadcasters, demonstrating CBS's strategy and the weaknesses of the noncommercial campaign. It is both troubling and ironic that Lee, in his work for a commercial radio network, was able to identify and articulate the core identity of nonprofit radio more effectively than its own representatives. That contemporary U.S. public broadcasting increasingly mirrors the language and behaviors of commercial broadcasters is even more problematic. The commercializing of public television's digital channels by some public broadcasters, coupled with the silence of those who oppose it, promotes a convergence of the public and commercial broadcasting sectors that is unhealthy for the public system and the people it serves. Blurring the lines of differentiation that make public television unique, this newest affiliation with the market reproduces the goals of Lee's 1934 campaign: to represent public television as invisible and unnecessary.

Section 307(c): Containing the Moment of Possibility

Back just days after Christmas recess in the winter of 1935, members of the 76th Congress learned the fate of nonprofit radio in an artfully ambiguous paragraph spliced between an appropriations bill for the executive office and legislation to regulate shipments of foreign oil. On January 21, 1935, the one-sentence, sixty-three-word entry in the *Congressional Record* reported only that the Federal Communications Commission was transmitting, "pursuant to law, a report containing certain recommendations, together with its reasons therefor, concerning the proposal that Congress, by statute, allocate fixed percentages of radio broadcasting facilities" to nonprofit radio. A digest of "hearings, etc., held by the Commission," and "the accompanying papers" were being referred to the Senate Committee on Interstate Commerce (*Cong. Rec.* 1935: 761). A similar report, half as long, was read in the House of Representatives the next day.

The seven-year battle for the control of U.S. airwaves was over. Begun in 1927 and concluded in the hearing rooms of a regulatory communications body comprised of appointed officials, the broadcast reform movement had taken its call for nonprofit radio to national conferences, committee hearings, and the Senate floor. It had introduced groundbreaking legislation in the Wagner-Hatfield Amendment by proposing not only that one fourth of all U.S. radio frequencies be allocated for noncommercial use, but also that nonprofit stations be allowed to sell airtime to pay their operating expenses (*Cong. Rec.* 1934: 8829). The radio reformers had made their appeals to national philanthropies, the popular press, the White House, and the public. The conversation that ensued was a broad discussion of radio and its purposes in a democratic society (McChesney 1993: 3). The tenets of broadcast reform sustained an engaged discursive moment involving many players and pulling from diverse sectors of American life. The discourse that resulted was massive, producing thousands of pages of official text, volumes of personal and professional correspondence, and numerous newspaper accounts, editorials, and letters to the editor.

Situated within this complicated conversation of official and popular discourse was the strategic planning document Lee developed for the commercial case against protected channels. Called in to produce the CBS presentation for the FCC hearings on Section 307(c), Lee was hardly a newcomer to corporate America. A powerful public relations strategist, his client list included, among many others, Bethlehem Steel, the Pennsylvania Railroad, Armour, Anaconda Copper, Interborough Rapid Transit Authority, and John D. Rockefeller (Lee Papers, summary 5–11). Lee was an avowed disciple of big business, and the campaign he developed for CBS in its fight against nonprofit radio was not a strategy of compromise or negotiation. He meant to win. And like other campaigns waged in the war against nonprofit broadcasters, this effort framed the fight as a battle over resources, to be fought not in the mainstream press, but rather behind the doors of a committee hearing room in Washington, D.C.

The success of the commercial broadcasters' campaign in the 1934 battle for frequency allocations has been documented, but it was not a given that nonprofit radio would lose this important contest over structural access to the public sphere. Broadcast reformers could have succeeded, at least partially, in their struggle for protected space on the radio spectrum. The fluidity of the Depression years, as well as the legislative precedents for resource protection under the New Deal, both suggest that Section 307(c) came before the American public in a moment conducive to social change.

Fluidity and Possibility

Although the thirties can be characterized as a decade of economic despair and national anxiousness, 1933 and 1934 sit within this larger landscape as a particularly fluid, volatile moment of American history. Taking office in March of 1933, Franklin Roosevelt had framed his presidential campaign in the rhetoric of economic reform. But at the close of the year, his promises of "social justice through social action" rang hollow for the millions of Americans still standing in soup lines, facing farm foreclosures, and struggling with personal issues of lost dignity, self-reliance, and self-respect. Despite the national euphoria accompanying Roosevelt's inauguration and the aggressive social legislation of the New Deal, the economy continued to dissolve. Marking the depths of the Depression, when almost fourteen million Americans were out of work, the years 1933 and 1934 were a point of societal rupture, a liminal moment when alternative discourses and concepts about the organization of cultural, political, and economic life had currency. The rhetoric of the left, surviving from the teens and twenties, and that of the broadcast reform movement, formally initiated in 1927 but framed within a twenty-year-old popular conversation about radio, ran headlong into a society that was coming apart at the seams. Old notions of progress, capitalism, and national identity floundered in a period of political turbulence, unrest, self-doubt, and widespread poverty.[1] By May of 1934 the situation was growing increasingly desperate. Americans were at a crossroads, bewildered by the rapid disintegration of the booming, seemingly prosperous society they had known in the 1920s. Ideas of community, cooperation, sacrifice, social-mindedness, tradition, and place came to the fore, as Americans sought out ways to weather the storm together (McElvaine 1993: xxiv). The tenets of nonprofit radio, with an emphasis on the public interest and welfare of the collective, would seem to cohere with the social currents driving much of American life. Among these commitments was broad support for the idea of the public good, demonstrated, in part, by a protected spectrum for nonprofit radio.

Set-Aside Legislation for Public Goods

Commitments to public life are the heart of resource preservation. Government protection of "public goods" was not new to Americans in 1934—the United States had long been a nation of public schools, public post offices, and public libraries—but the thirties witnessed even more public-oriented legislation. Over a five-year period, the New Deal ushered in measures protecting, funding, and/or setting aside resources as varied as public highways, public ranges, and public swimming pools in Washington, D.C. Protection was granted to navigable waters, watersheds, birds and their nests in the Canal Zone, government records, land in Superior National Forest, and the water supply of Ogden, Utah. Federal monies were allocated for the acquisition of lands for a public airfield in Yuma, Arizona, and for public buildings in Washington, D.C. (Sitkoff 1985: 57).

The New Deal's philosophy and practice of public goods and public interest also extended to agricultural conservation and federal patronage of the arts. Signed into law on May 12, 1933, the Agricultural Adjustment Act moved to take farmland out of cultivation, in part to control prices by limiting production (McElvaine 1993: 149). However, the farm legislation was also motivated by strong commitments to resource conservation. American farmland, though owned and operated as private property, was regarded as a national resource, and the New Deal farm bill put in place a series of practices that would ensure the protection of that resource through the systematic set-asides of farm acreage. During this period, FDR also endorsed a series of work programs that supported artists and their productions. Works Progress Administration (WPA) art, which focused on public works and arts for the people as a whole, put American aesthetic expression on the agenda as a national resource deserving of public protection and economic support (McElvaine 1993: 268).

The Paulist Father John B. Harney, testifying before the Senate Committee on Interstate Commerce in March 1934, called for similar protection of nonprofit radio. He proposed not only that 25 percent of all radio frequencies be set aside for noncommercial broadcasting, but that those frequencies should "not be the subject of barter or exchange but rather be reserved indefinitely, permanently, for associations that are carrying on this cultural work" (Senate 1934). As the superior general of New York City's Missionary Society of St. Paul the Apostle, Harney was an advocate for the order's nonprofit radio station, WLWL (McChesney 1993: 73); and the concept of "public goods" clearly motivated his stance with the SCIC. New Deal legislation designed to reserve, protect, and conserve other important resources, such as water, forests, wildlife, art, and historical documents, could reasonably have been summoned as legislative precedents for the set-aside of frequencies for nonprofit radio. Although FDR ultimately did not support Wagner-Hatfield (Blakely 1979: 65–66), the positioning of noncommercial radio as a national asset in need of federal patronage was consistent with the philosophies and practices of his administration. Clearly, the concepts of commonness, conservation, and community benefits applied to radio waves as well.

Historical Background: Broadcast Reform Movement

If Wagner-Hatfield and Section 307(c) developed in a moment of progressive possibility, they were also caught in a policy and regulation continuum that advanced the interests of commercial radio. A discussion of the 1930s spectrum debates must also examine the context of early radio and the events leading up to the 1934 FCC hearings. As Engelman (1996: 18) notes, the first American radio stations went on the air in late 1920, with rapid proliferation. The spectrum soon became overcrowded; by 1927, the number of stations in the United States had risen to 733 (Schmeckebier 1932: 4). This on-air congestion led to passage of the Radio Act of 1927, which created the Federal Radio Commission (FRC) and provided it with the mandate and the power to "clean up the airwaves" (McChesney 1993: 17).

Radio Act of 1927 and Broadcast Reform

Noncommercial radio, which previously had controlled roughly a third of the spectrum, changed dramatically with these developments. Most observers, past and present, would agree that radio broadcasting was out of control, that some ordered system was necessary for development of policies and practices that would meet public needs and aid the development of radio, and that the FRC was an agency that could conceivably organize the spectrum coherently. What was seen as problematic, however, was the commission's willingness to employ regulation and law to structure broadcasting to the benefit of commercial broadcasters and to the detriment and not infrequent demise of noncommercial stations. Nonprofit stations that had been operating for years on unlimited hours and open frequencies found themselves out of business in a new communications environment that privileged for-profit organizations and the radio networks.

It was this overt silencing of a once vibrant sector of American radio that gave rise to the broadcast reform movement in the United States. Bracketed historically between the Radio Act of 1927 and the Communications Act of 1934, the broadcast reform movement brought to the fore an unprecedented political debate about mass media in the United States (McChesney 1993: 3). The conversation involved a range of players, including educators, socialists, farmers, philanthropists, members of the general public, and religious, labor, arts, and civic leaders. They all supported some form of noncommercial broadcasting and the possibilities it suggested for diverse voices and participation.

WLWL went on the air on September 25, 1925, as a 5,000-watt station assigned to the 1040 frequency (McChesney 1987: 119). It was considered one of the twenty-five most powerful stations in the country (McChesney 1993: 73). In 1927, the FRC assigned WLWL to a new frequency, 810, which it would share with commercial station WMCA. WLWL was cut to two broadcast hours per day, with WMCA receiving the balance of the airtime (McChesney 1987:119). The Paulist Fathers refused to concede without a struggle. Over the next six years, Harney wrote numerous letters, made appeals to the FRC, mobilized a campaign that generated in one week 20,000 letters of support for increased airtime for WLWL, and tried generally to keep the station solvent (McChesney 1993:74). Finally, in March of 1934, Harney made his appearance before Congress, arguing that noncommercial radio should be granted a protected position through broadcasting policy and regulation (Engelman 1996: 33). His request failed in committee, but Harney persuaded the two

SCIC members who voted for the amendment, Robert Wagner (D-N.Y.) and Henry Hatfield (D-W.Va.), to take up the measure and present it from the floor of the U.S. Senate (McChesney 1999: 216). This effort produced the Wagner-Hatfield Amendment, proposed legislation that could have altered the structure of American broadcasting.

Wagner-Hatfield Amendment and Section 307(c)

The Wagner-Hatfield Amendment, the last large-scale, national attempt to provide protected spectrum for noncommercial radio, was introduced from the floor of the U.S. Senate on May 15, 1934. Wagner-Hatfield proposed that the newly created Federal Communications Commission void all radio licenses within 90 days (later amended to 180 days) and reallocate the airwaves. Had it passed, the Wagner-Hatfield Amendment would have set aside a fourth of all radio allocations for noncommercial use and granted those stations the right to sell airtime to pay their operating expenses (*Cong. Rec.* 1934: 8829). After four hours of debate, the amendment was defeated by a roll call vote of 42-23. Later that afternoon, legislation creating the Communications Act of 1934 and mandating the status quo for commercial broadcasting passed the Senate on a voice vote. In consideration of the substantial public support for a noncommercial set-aside, Congress offered a concession to broadcast reformers through Section 307(c). This amendment to the Communications Act of 1934 called for a regulatory study into the set-aside of channels for nonprofit radio (Engelman 1996: 35). The FCC was directed to conduct open hearings on the question of the feasibility and usefulness of the noncommercial set-aside.

Although noncommercial radio faced an unsympathetic FDR administration, a devastated economy, and the lack of a unifying network, there was nonetheless significant popular and legislative support for reserved nonprofit frequencies. Smulyan (1994: 112) notes that radio's increasing commercialization antagonized a number of listeners, who claimed advertising polluted the airwaves. This discontent with commercial radio translated into a public response that produced, almost overnight, more than 60,000 petition signatures and thousands of letters and telegrams in favor of the Wagner-Hatfield Amendment (McChesney 1993: 199). The supporters included, among many others, twenty-six members of Long Island's South Shore Players; the New

York Typographical Union No. 6, and fifty students from Niagara University, who claimed,

> Commercial broadcasting threatens to destroy a chief source of cultural education. Continuance of the present policy will constitute an irreparable loss to the American people. It will rob them of a chance for intellectual development; it shows a discrimination against the small radio station in favor of the rich, powerful 'chain stations'; it is a step in the curtailment of every citizen's freedom of speech. (Wagner Papers)

Emil Lange of Silver Creek, New York, wrote in favor of "free speech over the air as well as a free press," while Marie Lydon reported turning

> from one station to another seeking vainly some entertainment for the adult brain—only fifth rate comedians whose offerings could please only undeveloped minds and crooners are to be found. I beg you to show your approval of the struggle of these non-profit making associations to preserve their ideals of serving the public interest. (Wagner Papers)

Elsie Smith's telegram was short and to the point: "Give us freedom on the radio!" and John Gostyla and Andy Wajewoolka wrote in support of Polish radio broadcasting:

> As an American citizen shows his spirit for his country, America, so do we, as American citizens of Polish birth. Most likely, few people forget that the Polish people make up a fair part of the foreigners in the United States of America. We are writing to you to get your help to maintain Polish programs on the radio, not only in Brooklyn, but in other states in the Union. (Wagner Papers)

Neither the networks nor the commercially oriented trade press was oblivious to this grassroots support for noncommercial radio. As Variety reported on May 8, 1934,

> [The] Wagner-Hatfield Amendment, [the] most serious threat encountered in years of warfare with educational groups, has strong backing and was believed today to have better than a 50-50 chance of being

adopted. [The] Catholic church, National Grange, assorted radio-education groups, and many lesser but potent organizations are riding the bandwagon and threatening to apply heat to Senators who turn thumbs down on [the] scheme. ("Air Enemies Unite Forces" 1934)

The following week, James Hanley, member of the Federal Communications Commission, was quoted in the *New York Times* as calling for new radio allocations, "using as a yardstick in the New Deal the welfare of all listeners" ("Hanley Suggests a New Deal" 1934: 7). Later that summer, a letter to WOI/Ames general manager W. I. Griffith from station engineer Andy Woolfries suggested support for set-aside spectrum space was still active:

As you know, the Wagner Bill disigned [*sic*] to give 25% of available channels to educational and religious stations, showed surprising strength at the last session of Congress. The radio section of the Federal Communications Commission . . . is [*sic*] called for hearings to begin on October 1. This, of course, is exceedingly disquieting to commercial stations, since the allotment would be on a state quota basis (Hull Papers, box 1).

A concern that the FCC might reverse its earlier position and establish new set-aside policies favoring nonprofit radio prompted commercial broadcasters to mount a persuasive campaign to protect their interests. The case was prepared in various ways. McChesney (1993: 214) reports that CBS vice president Henry Bellows took a leave of absence to organize efforts for the trade organization National Association of Broadcasters. The National Broadcasting Company (NBC), seeking representation by a credible, seemingly detached "outside man," hired journalist William Hard as its formal spokesperson. CBS brought in Ivy Ledbetter Lee.

Lees's Campaign: A Seamless Fit with the Status Quo

Ewen (1996: 78) writes that Lee was most often hired in a crisis situation to perform "damage control." Such was certainly the case when he represented the Rockefeller family and the Colorado Iron and Fuel Company after fourteen striking miners, miners' wives, and children were killed in the Ludlow Massacre of 1914. Hired by the Rockefellers to "secure publicity for their views," Lee produced a series of pamphlets that claimed to tell the facts about the massacre, but were, in Ewan's terms, "routine . . . exaggerations and juicy denunciations" (1996: 79). More often than not, Lee engineered the facts to present a selective truth on behalf of his corporate clients. This is further shown in Lee's own words. In 1916 he spoke before the American Electric Railway Association:

> It is not the facts alone that strike the popular mind, but the way in which they take place and in which they are published that kindle the imagination. . . . Besides, what is a fact? The effort to state an absolute fact is simply an attempt to . . . give you my interpretation of the facts (Lee Papers, packet 1, folder 1, box 1).

The campaign Lee developed for CBS in its fight against nonprofit radio was not a strategy of compromise or negotiation. He meant to ut-terly defeat the opposition, and his campaign tactics included "rein-terpretation" of the facts. In very specific ways, Lee reframed the cen-tral issues, questions, and definitions of the noncommercial set-aside debate. Employing a method of reversal and appropriation, he not only cast his client, CBS, as a noncommercial broadcaster dedicated to pub-lic service, but he discounted broadcast reformers as inept and unde-serving. Importantly, he appropriated–and then reinvented—the broadcast reform movement's conceptual base. The basic goals of this campaign were delineated in the following three-point plan:

> The first object of the presentation must be to show that Columbia pro-grams, broadcast by Columbia controlled stations, are *so well serving the public interest, convenience and necessity that no special orders from the Commission could serve to improve them.*
>
> The second object would be to show—largely by inference—that *public interest, convenience, and necessity would actually be damaged if any broadcasting channels or time were withdrawn* from these stations.
>
> The third object must be to indicate—almost solely through infer-ence—such an *excellence of service among all stations under Columbia con-trol that Columbia's performance will serve as an actual standard of judgment* for the Commission (Lee Papers, box 57; italics added.)

Bitzer (1968: 3-4) has characterized the rhetorical situation as hav-ing five major components: rhetor, speech, audience, exigence, and constraints. Despite comments by critics that Bitzer's model takes an especially narrow view of speaker, audience, and context, his paradigm seems useful in analyzing how Lee construed the setting in which he developed arguments for CBS. Of special interest are ways in which Lee redefined the rhetorical situation through a new interpretation of "exigence." Seen as the challenge or purpose of the discourse, exigence in the 1934 FCC hearings became, in Lee's campaign, not a debate over spectrum policy, but rather a discussion of program types. His first move in accomplishing this turn was to engineer the language of the amendment. "Section 307 seems to have been purposely phrased in vague terminology," he noted in his memo regarding the FCC presentation (Lee Papers, box 57). With that strategic insight, the first sentence of his campaign plan, Lee proceeded to flip terms, meanings, and arguments to suit the needs of CBS. Public became private; facilities were activities; market interest replaced public interest; and noncommercial radio was eclipsed by its collapse into commercial practice.

Lee's strategy was rhetorical, calculated to meld the genre, institutional identity, and public interest objectives of nonprofit radio into existing commercial broadcasting structures and practice. Commercial broadcasters, and CBS in particular, said Lee, should be shown to already broadcast a large percentage of "'non-profit' or noncommercial programs of a high cultural level, thus making it unnecessary to issue a special order requiring them to do just what they are doing" (Lee Papers, box 57).

A month later, speaking from a crisp text conceived and written by Lee, CBS's Paley depicted the network as the best of both commercial and noncommercial broadcasting. Testifying in FCC allocation hearings on October 17, 1934, Paley called CBS a "sound business enterprise" and a national resource dedicated to "mass education and culture." He reported that during the first nine months of 1934, only 31 percent of the network's programming had been "commercial radio." The other 69 percent, comprised of "3,011 hours of non-commercial broadcasts," was "educational, cultural, informative, and religious." This part of the schedule, "non-revenue producing and sponsored by Columbia at its own expense," was evidence, said Paley, of the network's commitments not only to the programming but also to the constituencies of nonprofit radio (Paley 1934: 2–3).

Lee's plan also developed the idea that the public interest, convenience, and necessity would actually be damaged by a change in the status quo. Not only would public access to the already excellent offerings of commercial radio be reduced, he argued, but the set-aside of frequencies for noncommercial radio would promote conflict among nonprofit groups: "The rivalry among religious orders and other organizations to secure desirable channels would stir up much bitterness, wholly contrary to the public interest." Lee also questioned how placing "desirable wave lengths in the hands of organizations often without sufficient revenues to maintain programs" could serve the public interest: "The past history of stations and wave lengths operated by religious, educational and labor organizations on a non-profit basis indicates that the programs so offered were of no higher cultural order, and often were of lesser public interest, than programs of the so-called 'commercial' stations" (Lee Papers, box 57). Opposition to nonprofit stations in profit-making activity—key to commercial broadcasting's attack on the Wagner-Hatfield Amendment just three months before—also emerged in Lee's campaign text. Could such stations, operated by "certain 'nonprofit' organizations" desiring "to make a profit to support their work" actually be considered nonprofit? "Presumably not," said Lee, suggesting the notion of a nonprofit organization using a "public utility to make profits sufficient to support its private work" would be "an extremely dangerous precedent for any national government." Prohibition of advertising sales was the only solution protecting the public from such a danger, "thus depriving these stations of revenue" and resulting in noncommercial stations too poverty-stricken to operate in the public interest. Lee closed this section of the text by suggesting the set-aside for nonprofit radio would actually benefit only those "philanthropic and educational organizations already so heavily endowed and so wealthy that they could bear the expense" of operating a nonprofit station, "with the result that many worthy causes not so long-established or so wealthy would be discriminated against" (Lee Papers, box 57).

Although Lee's campaign did not directly address the FRC's previous rulings on "propaganda" stations, his understanding of this agency position flavored the language and strategy of the text Paley delivered before the FCC. In granting frequency allocations over the previous seven years, the FRC had consistently privileged commercial over nonprofit interests on the question of bias, saying capitalist broadcasters were more objective due to their lack of commitments to anything beyond monetary gain. In the radio business solely to make a profit, these commercial broadcasters could be trusted, said the FRC, to avoid propaganda and special interest viewpoints. "There is no room in the broadcast band for every school of thought, religious, political, social, and economic, each to have its separate broadcasting station, its mouthpiece in the ether," declared the FRC in 1927 (qtd. in McChesney 1993: 27). Since not every group could have a mouthpiece, none would; and the marketplace would come to be seen as the arbiter of fairness, protecting American society from the overtly ideological and the minority interest.

The most important move Lee made in defense of the status quo, however, was to interpret Section 307(c) as a congressional mandate for the study of nonprofit "activities," rather than nonprofit "facilities." The set-aside of facilities, or radio frequencies, was the goal of Wagner-Hatfield supporters, and a study of such resources was the compromise they expected from the FCC. In moving from facilities—by which, Lee noted in his memorandum, "Father Harney undoubtedly meant to construe 'wave lengths'"—to activities, Lee changed the stakes of the debate, evacuating the political and economic intent of Section 307(c). By reframing the language of this section of the Communications Act of 1934, and by casting CBS as the exemplar of radio programming, Lee altered the parameters of inquiry (what questions would be asked) and legitimacy (who would be believed), effectively negating broadcast reformers' demands for channels of their own. The investigation of the set-aside became a nonissue.

A Fragmented Response by Reformers

Lee's campaign was an important component in the defeat of the noncommercial set-aside. His well-organized program stood in sharp contrast to the aimless discourse of the reformers. Not only was Lee's project organized and focused, but it also had the clear support of other commercial broadcasters offering similar evidence. Most important, however, was Lee's programmatic effort to defend his client and discount his opponent. Lee's campaign changed an investigation of spectrum assets into talk about radio programs. In the end, Lee's rhetorical strategy of appropriation and reversal turned the broadcast reformers' premises against themselves and employed their claims as justification and support for his own client's position.

The hearings on the nonprofit set-aside were conducted from mid-October through mid-November 1934. By the time FCC chairman

Eugene O. Sykes called for the official vote, more than 100 witnesses had testified, producing almost 14,000 pages of text. The evidence presented was overwhelmingly in favor of commercial broadcasting. Commercial radio's argument was coherent and persuasive, with 72 expert witnesses representing education and the arts, statements from 286 commercial stations pledging their commitment to quality programming, and a temperate and convincing defense of the status quo by network executives. The positions taken by broadcast reformers, on the other hand, were wholly disorganized and fragmented. The first three days of testimony, ostensibly by witnesses favoring the set-aside for noncommercial broadcasting, offered up a range of ideas about nonprofit radio but few arguments for reserved channels. Over the course of the hearings, as many as nine different proposals were presented by nonprofit broadcasters, and more than a third of their witnesses simply did not show up to testify (McChesney 1993: 215–16; Engelman 1996: 35). A coalition plagued from its inception by a lack of organization, coherent vision, and street-fighting savvy, the movement for broadcast reform finally disintegrated. Unable to withstand the onslaught of a persuasive network campaign and its own lack of institutional vision, nonprofit radio was relegated to the margins, where it was defined as invisible, unnecessary, and financially impossible.

The quashing of Section 307(c) and the resounding defeat of the noncommercial set-aside would seem the logical termination to a political timeline that began in 1927 with the FRC's campaign to "clean up the airwaves." Of the 200 noncommercial radio stations broadcasting in 1927, only sixty-five were still on the air in 1934, and they provided but 2 percent of total U.S. broadcast time (Engelman 1996: 37; McChesney 1993: 30–31). Further, the years 1932–35 saw federal statute officially establish the rules and conditions by which a network-dominated and advertiser-supported funding paradigm became entrenched in American cultural life. As this broadcasting system gained cultural acceptance, it also came of age financially. In January 1935, *Variety* reported gross earnings of $42,888,730 in 1934 for the networks and a 44 percent increase in profits for CBS (*Variety*, January 15, 1935). Finally the FCC established the ascendancy of the commercial sector in terms of spectrum use, suggesting that educators learn to cooperate with commercial broadcasters within the existing system.

There is evidence that the social moment in which the discourse and practice of broadcast reform developed was conducive to social change. The thirties was a point of social rupture when old ideas about community and new ones about the social uses of mass media could have flourished side by side. These years also saw unprecedented legislative protection for public resources, which could have legitimately been extended to set-aside allocations and protected funding for noncommercial broadcasting. Further, the mid-thirties provided a cultural environment in which thousands of Americans were engaged in an energetic conversation about radio—pulling 1,200 people each summer to Columbus, Ohio, for the annual Institute for Education by Radio (J. Robertson 1981: 7), attracting more than a hundred educators to a national conference on the "use of radio as a cultural agency in a democracy" ("U.S. Radio System" 1934: 16), earning organized labor's support for a 50 percent set-aside for nonprofit radio in a San Francisco conference of the AFL (McChesney 1993: 220), and producing volumes of text in the popular press.

Even as the public discussed radio's potential as a social good, however, the political maneuvering of a small group of men in Washington pushed American broadcasting relentlessly toward a future framed within the economic structure and programming practices of for-profit media. Meeting in committee, powerful individuals such as Clarence Dill, chairman of the Senate Committee on Interstate Commerce, and Eugene O. Sykes of the FCC set the rules, contained the discourse, and called for a vote. In each case, the result was the denial of radio frequencies for nonprofit media.

The contest over spectrum control not only set in place a policy that effectively denied noncommercial radio access to the AM band for the long term, but cemented a for-profit economic structure for U.S. broadcasting. Importantly, this loss for public media also established powerful parameters for public broadcasting's future defense of public channels, encoding the system's silences about diverse spectrum control as an enduring argument for mainstream public speech.

This is not to suggest that some noncommercial broadcasters did not offer compelling concepts about spectrum preservation and use. The record shows that useful ideas about broadcasting surfaced, for example, when Henry Ewbank took the stand for the National Association of College and University Broadcasting Stations:

You [the FCC] are the planners. We are asking you to provide for the public interests as you draw up your proposals for submission to our next congress.

We in the United States have always been slow to conserve the public interests in what was once public domain. We have squandered our oil and our coal and our forests, until we have come to the point of asking our government to set out little trees so that our children may know what a tree is like. Fortunately the situation in radio is not quite analogous, since the radio channels do remain public property. But you have a real opportunity to conserve for the public interest the greatest discovery since the invention of the printing press, a means of education fully as important to our civilization as coal or gasoline or lumber (FCC 1950: 16).

Similarly, Alice Keith, a pioneer in educational radio, argued "control of [the] budget should be in the hands of those whose motives are primarily social and not commercial" (qtd. in McChesney 1993: 222). Another reformer, Dr. Floyd Reeves of the Tennessee Valley Authority, called for creation of a federally subsidized noncommercial "chain" to supplement the offerings of commercial radio (McChesney 1993: 217). These progressive voices carried a common pro-social theme and were obviously motivated by obligations to the public good. Regrettably, the absence of clearly delineated commitments to the specific goals of democratic media blunted their effectiveness.

The salient issue in 1934 was spectrum control, and as the national conversation opened to a discussion of the airwaves, noncommercial broadcasters had the opportunity to press for an ownership structure that granted access, use, and control of frequencies to a range of constituencies. Lacking substantive commitments to popular voices and a solid plan, however, nonprofit radio could not develop or sustain a powerful, persuasive argument for public channels. Ironically, the hearings' most eloquent witness for popular access to radio may have been CBS's Paley, who appropriated ideas of a participatory public to cement the dominance of for-profit media:

Educational, informative, and generally cultural programs have played a large part in these broadcasts which have attracted and held our millions of listeners. They are not there because they elevate and improve people's minds, according to special standards prescribed by radio executives. They are there, rather, because they reflect the interests of a very important number of groups in the community. They are there because our constant policy is to give such groups a voice, and these groups cooperate with us constantly in creating these programs (Paley 1934: 5).

There are startling similarities between the opportunities, challenges, and compromise positions for noncommercial media in 1934 and today. McChesney (1993) has described the seven-year window of opportunity that opened from 1927 to 1934, allowing vigorous public debate on the purpose and ownership of radio. Radio was seen by many as a social force, and the spectrum was perceived as a public resource. A space was held open—largely through the efforts of the Payne Fund and other dedicated broadcast reformers—for progressive speech and social action. It was within this zone of possibility that noncommercial broadcasters battled for a broadcasting system structured to advance the public good. The skill, resources, and political power of the commercial sector, as well as the cautious fumbling of the noncommercial broadcasters, were contributing factors in the ultimate development of a network-dominated, advertiser-driven media system in the U.S. This tragedy notwithstanding, the opportunities of the moment, to enlarge the public sphere and develop a robust and substantive institutional character for noncommercial radio, were immense.

Today, the digital revolution offers similar kinds of opportunities for the American public and U.S. public broadcasting. As in the 1920s and 1930s, emergent technology has produced the conditions by which public space can be reserved for discussion and performance. Such a free zone for problem-solving discourse, with its potential for enlarging the civic participation of U.S. citizens, can only be useful. Clearly, the possibilities exist to define a part of the digital spectrum as public, not commercial, and to ascribe its use as public service broadcasting. The prospects for creative use of this resource are significant; they range from performances by kids to stories by Native elders to discourse by social movement activists. It is troubling, then, that the FCC (at the behest of public television lobbyists) has elected to grant public broadcasters the right to commercialize the digital channels assigned to them. The October 11, 2001, FCC decision gave public stations "flexibility" in determining the use of their digital channels ("Public Television Stations"). Although public broadcasters must provide one free video programming stream and pursue a "primarily educational" service on ancillary spectrum, they are free to use the "excess spectrum" (which may amount to as many as five other channels) as they choose, including a variety of profit-centered activities (Odenwald 2001: 1).

Critics of the decision fear an increased slide toward overall commercialization of the public system. Spokespersons for the Media Access Project and Citizens for Independent Public Broadcasting (CIPB) have voiced concern that public TV will be unalterably changed through such a close and accepted relationship with the market. Commissioner Michael J. Copps, the lone dissenter in the FCC vote, suggests that the decision may very well cost public television its core identity:

> Public television is about serving the better angels of our nature. It is about sustaining the virtues of education, civic involvement, and American democracy. . . . Public television is supposed to be, and is, different [from commercial television]. When it begins to lose this different identity, it begins to lose its soul (Copps 2001).

CIPB's founder, Jerrold Starr, has been especially troubled by the vagueness of the educational requirement for public television's supplementary services. Should public TV finally opt to divide its DTV channels into six multicast streams, Starr predicts that at least two of them will be leased for profit (see Odenwald 2001: 3).

The use of public channels for market-driven activity is still being debated within PTV. Although some stations have outlined plans to use digital spectrum for profit, most have not; and there is evidence that as many as a third of public broadcasting stations do not currently intend to use any of their digital channels for non-mission-related services (G. Collins 1999: 2). Even so, the most vocal stance is that favoring a partial commercialization of the public digital spectrum, and the debate increasingly mirrors the language of commercial broadcasting. In early 1999, a venture capitalist brought in to help public broadcasting executives evaluate the potential "entrepreneurial uses" of public channels exulted, "You guys are holding on to very valuable real estate!" He urged public media to establish market share early on and said he saw no danger of there being unused DTV transmission capacity: "Having too much bandwidth is like being too rich or too beautiful." Station managers reported appreciation for his approach. One observed, "He speaks my language. He's telling us, 'Guys, you've got unused assets out here. You've got to figure out how to leverage your assets. You'd better learn to 'ready, shoot, aim!'" ("Station Execs" 1999).

This language of the market, and the goals and values it demonstrates, are inconsistent with the long-standing objectives of public television and are not useful in articulating a public mission for the twenty-first century. The commercial model has rarely worked for the advancement of alternative texts and projects for underserved audiences, and its application now has serious ramifications for the viability of broadcasting in the public interest. At the very least, this move to commercialize public channels distracts public television professionals from their central project: the virtues of education, civic involvement, and American democracy. At the worst, it furthers the deterioration of noncommercial broadcasting's public purpose and facilitates the system's convergence with commercialized media.

This brings to mind John Harney, who, caught between a rock and a hard place, lobbied for the right to sell advertising to support WLWL in 1934. Lacking public resources and a vocabulary to argue for them, he chose the dominant commercial model to support the public service activities of his parish's radio station. The tactic backfired, as opponents in Congress used it to discredit his project. They, like Ivy Lee, questioned if "certain 'non-profit' organizations" desiring "to make a profit to support their work" could actually be considered nonprofit. Their answer, like Lee's, was, "Presumably not." Public broadcasting will undoubtedly face similar problems by selling time (however configured) on the digital channels it controls. In fact, legislation advocating a cut of $12 million from CPB digital funding was proposed the day the FCC decision was announced. The bill's sponsor, Rep. Cliff Stearns (R-Fla.), suggested that public stations' newly acquired ability to raise money made them less in need of federal funding (Odenwald 2001: 3).

Harney's 1934 proposal of advertising sales by a noncommercial station was a fallback measure taken up out of desperation. Public broadcasting can ill afford a similar desperate response to its needs for funding. Too much is at stake, including the nation's perceptions of the system and public broadcasting's own institutional culture. Public broadcasters could better, and more profitably, spend their time and human resources in creative program design and efforts to cultivate a climate of publicness in U.S. culture. Indeed the idea of "excess spectrum" is antithetical to the broad public service that stations could and should be providing for their audiences. In an age of narrow—and narrowing—broadcast possibilities for inner city youth, Mexican Americans, gays and lesbians, the elderly, noncentrist politicos, and other constituency groups, there is clear need for all the spectrum public media can acquire. Even so, public broadcasters have long demonstrated a lack of creativity in their use of spectrum. Instead of developing stations that target the diverse and multivocal talk of its neighborhoods, the public system has consistently—even on second channels and overlapping stations—cultivated a public television taste community that agrees to tune in for eight hours each month. Strong paradigms of constituency diversity and minority service are available in European public media, and PTV leader Hartford Gunn proposed a multichannel system for U.S. public television in the early 1980s.[2] Models exist for a more imaginative and audience-based approach to spectrum use. That public television professionals have not explored new strategies, and may now be turning to a commercial use of the public's spectrum, is evidence of a severely limited public mission.

It is telling that Douglas Kellner's (2001) recent discussion of progressive media includes community radio, public access televison, and the Internet, but does not even mention public broadcasting. A deeply internalized and clearly articulated public mission could establish an active presence for public broadcasting in the public sphere. Lacking genuine commitments to the performance of public service work—which is, at its heart, noncommercial—U.S. public broadcasting's wagon seems hitched instead to the goals and values of commercial media. It is deeply ironic that the claims Ivy Lee made in 1934, as he collapsed the identities of nonprofit and network media and cast CBS as the best of noncommercial radio, seem to have surfaced, in reverse, some seventy years later.

Notes

1. By late 1933, the country's GNP had dropped 29 percent from the peak of prosperity in 1929. Consumption expenditures were down by 18 percent, construction by 78 percent, investment by 98 percent (McElvaine 1993: 75). Thirty-eight states had closed their banks; nine million savings

accounts had been lost; the suicide rate was up 25 percent (Bauman and Coode 1988: 5). U. S. Steel's 1929 payroll of 225,000 full-time workers fell to almost zero in early 1933. Throughout the East, women lucky enough to still be working in the garment trades earned less than $5 a week (Levine 1988: 50). Almost 700,000 Ohioans were unemployed, and in some counties more than 70 percent of the population was on the welfare rolls. The Chicago Building Trades Council, which had seen 30,000 carpenters, 22,000 painters, and 73,000 other construction workers employed before the crash, found only 10,000 working regularly in 1933 (Bauman and Coode 1988: 41).

In the West, Colorado's per capita income fell by a third; employment in Montana's mining industry plummeted by 60 percent, and New Mexico's agricultural crop dropped in value from $40 million in 1929 to $9.5 million in 1933 (Bauman and Coode 1988: 5). Among those hardest hit by the collapse of the national economic system were farmers, who were virtually bankrupt by the time Roosevelt took office in March of 1933. Over a four-year period, total farm income had plunged 60 percent, from $13 billion in 1929 to $5.5 billion in 1933. Farm prices declined drastically during that span, dropping 61 percent overall and taking the price of wheat from $100 a bushel to $19.23. Cotton fell from twenty cents a pound to six cents. Unable to meet mortgage and tax payments on their property, farmers across the country lost their land and homes to foreclosure. Incredibly, a fourth of rural Mississippi was sold at auction on one single day in April 1932, and the following year would bring the foreclosure of 60 percent of farms in North Dakota (Mertz 1978: 65; Bauman and Coode 1988: 3).

Poverty, long a feature of rural Southern life, magnified as the Depression deepened. By 1933, 60,000 Southern farmers had lost their land, and per capita income in Louisiana, like most of the South, was cut in half between 1929 and 1933. Poor health, inadequate medical care, and hunger were rampant throughout the region; February 1934 found Florida with 90,000 malaria patients and 250,000 cases of hookworm. In June 1933, Henry Wallace, Roosevelt's new secretary of agriculture, received a letter describing the living and working conditions of Mississippi's black sharecroppers, who were staying alive by eating oats processed and sold as mule feed (Mertz 1978: 1, 13, 51).

2. A plan for multiple program services for U.S. public television was developed by a task force of PTV programming and management executives in May 1979. Three services—identified as "Blue," "Red," and "Green"—would have addressed different audiences and programming objectives. Each was to have singular missions of service, commitments to system-wide diversity of editorial outlook and control, and separate structures for management, staffing,

and financing. The Blue network was seen as the "lead" service, offering high-quality prime-time programs in the arts and public affairs. The Red service was intended to comprise special-interest, minority, and community programs, including sports, experimental projects, and interactive discussions. The Green network would have featured educational programming for in-school and home audiences, including children's programs, instructional shows for classrooms, adult education, college for-credit courses, "how-to" programs, language studies, and personal-improvement programming (Gunn 1980: 37–44). Implementation of the proposal was hindered by federal budget cuts in the early 1980s.

CHAPTER THREE

Domestications of the Hearth: The Battle for Educational Frequencies in 1950–51

Taking its cues from the homebound postwar culture of the 1950s, noncommercial TV developed at the intersections of domestic bliss and a nationwide silencing of dissident speech. Pinioned between two dominant ideological social forces, educational television evolved to satisfy them both. The 1950–51 battle for educational channels produced 914 oral and written statements, secured 11.7 percent of the spectrum for public broadcasting, and ushered in a television system dedicated to formal, in-school instruction. After two years of campaign planning, the result was a compromise that restricted noncommercial broadcasting's sphere of influence largely to the classroom and silenced much of its progressive potential.

This whittling away of public media purpose had its origins in the spectrum fights of the thirties. Two years after Wagner-Hatfield cemented a for-profit, advertiser-driven economic structure for U.S. broadcasting, the National Committee on Education by Radio (NCER) announced it would accept the status quo and cooperate with commercial broadcasters and the FCC (Hill 1942: 72). By this time, other broadcast reform groups had largely collapsed, although the Paulist Fathers continued their efforts to stay solvent and regain full-time status on the air. Finally, in 1937, when all applications to the FCC for a clear-channel license had been denied and it became apparent that WLWL could not survive, John Harney's station sold for a pittance of his parish's investment (McChesney 1993: 228).[1] WCFL, the Voice of Labor, had been acquired by NBC in 1934 (McChesney 1993: 146); and the thirty-five educational stations left on the air struggled to endure the rest of the Depression.

Lacking frequencies, facilities, funding, and leadership, the broadcast reform movement seemed to die a quiet and insignificant death. After more than twenty years of engaged public talk about mass media's potential to enliven and invigorate social life, nonprofit radio's discussion of publicness and community was still. The FCC ruling on January 21, 1935—brief but ambiguous—was underpinned by assumptions that commercial broadcasting was able and willing to perform some of the tasks of nonprofit radio. In the end, it did not; and a silence that had previously embodied absence, closure, and termination emerged as a moment of possibility. In 1950–51, as the country worried about Communism, Korea, the bomb, large organizations, television, and its children, an old conversation about control of the airwaves came to the fore again. This time nonprofit broadcasters were ready, claiming 242 reserved frequencies for educational TV.

This plea for instructional channels for American schoolchildren was a lively and passionate discourse by educators who believed U.S. education would be markedly improved through the use of television technology. Many were convinced that their efforts were nonprofit television's last chance for spectrum space, and they joined in a successful effort to produce the framework for today's public television channels. Even so, the strategic decision by the Joint Committee on Educational Television (JCET) and the National Association of Educational Broadcasters (NAEB) to promote a specialized, in-school use of noncommercial TV abandoned other constituencies and narrowly defined educational television as instructional. A public service became a teaching tool; the cost was a public mission, a broad-based audience, and an enduring institutional identity. Writing in 1993, Williard Rowland observed:

As late as the early 1990s, there remained little evidence of public broadcasting leaders (including board members, chief executives, senior managers, and producers in the various national, regional, and local station organizations) being able to write or speak at length and in depth about the philosophy, history, and social expectations of their institution, let alone the broader realm of related questions about its role in American culture, politics, and social order. (167)

This indecision and lack of purpose by U.S. public broadcasters has its roots in the choices made, in part, by broadcast reformers in the fall of 1950. The allocation hearings of 1950–51 offered a rare opportunity for national examination of U.S. broadcasting practice, policy, and structure. Listener groups were forming, mothers were writing letters to the FCC, and newspaper columnists continually offered critique of educational radio and commercial television. A popular discourse about culture and communication had emerged, and a nation was listening as broadcast reformers and FCC commissioners gathered to chart the future of educational television. Educational broadcasters' decision to settle for a depoliticized, school-centered, and distinctly secondary public television system cut this conversation short, truncating noncommercial broadcasting's public mission and crippling its internalized sense of confidence and purpose.

A central purpose of this chapter is to define the social and political moment in which educational TV channels were allocated and to explore how dominant social forces of the 1950s helped determine the shape of U.S. noncommercial televison. The educational model—tied to values of privacy, home, service to children, and national security— acted to constrain the public potential of noncommercial broadcasting. Developed under the invisible pressures of postwar domestic life, the system's family-values paradigm was also a compromise hammered out in a social landscape of paranoia and anxiety about loyalty oaths and the Cold War. Notions of a lively, combative public were clearly at risk during this period of American history (L. May 1989: 146); and what survived as noncommercial broadcasting was, in part, what could be negotiated in a difficult moment of rigid gender roles, discourses of suburbia, and the Red Scare.

This is not to suggest that noncommercial media's "educational compromise" resulted entirely from the social context in which the frequencies were allocated. Certainly, other factors, including the economic structure of U.S. broadcasting and the industry's own history of ambivalence about broad public work, framed choices made by noncommercial broadcasters in 1950–51. However, focusing on the response of 1950s broadcast reformers to their social environment can offer insights into how the movement's rhetorical arguments and political strategies not only resulted in an instructional model for noncommercial broadcasting in the short term, but advanced an organizational culture that continues to stymie progressive action by public broadcasting.

Also, as a rich and lively debate produced by committed education professionals, testimony at the FCC hearings stands as proof entered into evidence of educational broadcasting's claim to frequencies. These portions of the record—specifically, reformers' arguments for spectrum space—provide a slice of a largely unrecorded piece of broadcast history produced by a group of people whose names and faces have been forgotten. The recovery of their voices seems useful. At the same time, in efforts to present a case they could win, noncommercial broadcasters made choices that privileged instructional rhetoric, excluded speakers from the social and political margins, and constructed an audience partial to mainstream expectations of school and TV.

The Fifties Family: Safety from War Abroad and Ruin Within

The early 1950s saw a boom in weddings and births. Reversing a century-long decline in the U.S. birthrate, postwar Americans established a pattern of early marriage and large families that held through the early sixties.[2] Some scholars suggest the success of fifties marriages was tied inextricably to their perceived ability to comfort and protect spouses and children in an "age of anxiety." Despite a nostalgia that would later depict the fifties as idyllic years of hoola hoops, sock hops, and poodle skirts, this decade was in fact an era of national fear and insecurity. Exhausted by sixteen long years of economic depression and global war and eager for respite, Americans found themselves living in a world threatened by McCarthyism, Communism, polio, and the bomb. The safe harbor promised by enemy surrender aboard the USS Missouri had not been forthcoming, and as the nation entered the fifties, political rhetoric fanned the flames of paranoia about communist infiltration in American life. Adlai Stevenson, in his race for the presidency in 1952, declared, "We cannot let our guard drop even for a moment. The only assumption is that no place is safe" (Carter 1983: 13).

The bomb that brought an end to World War II ushered in the Cold War, and while politicians fretted over Soviet secret agents burrowed like moles into U.S. society, American soldiers were fighting and dying again, this time in Korea. A police action became a prolonged conflict, one the country couldn't seem to win, and the jaunty self-confidence Americans had known at the end of World War II took on new shades of doubt. In the last analysis, wide-scale war was averted. On July 27, 1953, after thirty-seven months of fighting and two million deaths—80 percent of them civilians—the United Nations negotiated a tenuous peace (Carter 1983: 56). Even so, the threat of a thermonuclear holocaust seemed a real and present danger for most American families, for if America had the bomb, so did the Russians. A technological wonder had become a threat to world existence.

The 1950s' family-centered culture also took shape amid the anticommunist witch hunts of the House Un-American Activities Committee (HUAC) and the FBI. The rhetoric and tactics of Joseph McCarthy created a climate of fear, as the Republican senator from Wisconsin produced lists of Reds in education, entertainment, religion, the military, and the government. He spoke of spies throughout the country, in every sector, and announced a vigilance to ferret them out. The social effects of McCarthyism were profound, working to pit neighbors and colleagues against one another and to silence voices of dissent in America.[3] Sigmund Diamond writes that some Americans, including university presidents and deans, joined McCarthy in stigmatizing alternatives to existing national policy as subversive, "sometimes out of agreement, sometimes hopeful that a display of bloodlust would buy immunity for them" (1992: 3–4). In other cases, Americans feared judgment of treason through association. In December 1953, in the midst of national efforts by the Immigration and Naturalization Service and the FBI to deport foreign-born citizens, I. F. Stone's *Weekly* noted: "The suffering in terms of broken families and disrupted lives is beyond the most sympathetic imagination. As serious is the moral degradation imposed by spreading terror. People are afraid to look lest they be tempted to help, and bring down suspicion on themselves" (Stone 1963: 35).

McCarthy and J. Edgar Hoover used the resources under their control to silence alternative, radical, liberal, and progressive discourses in an overtly ideological war on difference and dissent in America. The effect was a narrowing of acceptable discourse and an intimidation of artists, writers, teachers, labor leaders, broadcasters, and political activists.

The ideology of the 1950s family, then, was as much about safety in the world as it was about domestic satisfaction. If victory in war could not provide a sense of security for the American citizenry, promises of abundance and family ties could. The home stood as a physical and psychological fortress against illicit sexuality, suicide, juvenile delinquency, and nuclear war; it provided security in a world that threatened, almost at any moment, to blow apart. Suburban family culture—romanticized on the weekly sitcom *Father Knows Best*, with shady streets, white ruffled curtains, and friendly neighborliness—seemed a safe refuge indeed from the ravages of war abroad and ruin within.

This was also the social environment in which noncommercial television presented its case and achieved a presence, however marginalized, on the radio spectrum. The space in which arguments for educational television frequencies developed was tied directly to the FCC's "freeze" on television licenses, announced on September 29, 1948. The large number of commercial applicants, reception interference among competing signals, and questions about color television led the FCC to put all applications for television licenses on hold. This hiatus, which ultimately lasted four years and entrenched the monopoly of CBS and NBC on the commercial side (Boddy 1990: 51), also granted nonprofit broadcasters time to design a strategic campaign for educational channels. Fueled philosophically by "vision seminars" sponsored by the Rockefeller Foundation and coordinated by the JCET, the project was to articulate a coherent argument for noncommercial allocations and recruit witnesses to support it. The effort was directed by I. Keith Tyler, on loan from the Bureau of Educational Research at Ohio State University (Blakely 1979: 9–14).

The FCC convened from November 27 to December 8, 1950, to hear reformers' testimony advocating set-aside space on the spectrum for educational television. Frieda Hennock, the commission's most ardent supporter of noncommercial broadcasting, produced a bundle of unsolicited mail to support her position. Those letters, components of a campaign that put seventy-six witnesses on the stand in favor of public media, were by women. Handwritten, many on personalized notepaper, more than half from women who identified themselves as "Mrs.," these letters brought a scathing assessment of commercial broadcasting. Three major lines of critique emerged: inferior quality of commercial programs, intrusive and adverse impacts of advertising, and television's potential to educate American children. Almost all requested dedicated channels for the instruction of children. One letter read, "If one citizen's approval can help you . . . lift the U.S. above the mental level of Howdy-Doody, here it is." Mary L. Sanders of Tuckahoe, New York, noted, "The T.V. advertising has reached a new low. My son took his T.V. set to the attic this fall." From Flushing, New York, came this short note: "We the Mothers' Club of P.S. 24 feel one Channel of Television should be kept open for educational purposes." Mrs. Donnell J. Smith of Arlington, Virginia, wrote: "This would constitute a very worthwhile step to counteract the growing commercialism which will ultimately affect the thinking of children and adults alike until we are all going around with dollar signs reflected in the pupils of our eyes." Writing from Milwaukee, M. Stewart said, "I for one don't want to be put in that stupid percentage who aren't interested in anything but comedy, variety, and crime. Let's raise the level!" Only one letter—of 544—specifically addressed the issue of broadcasting and public life. Marjorie F. Warner wrote, "America's citizenship has much at stake in your campaign" ("Hennock Papers"). A discourse on home, school, child, and viewing, these letters spoke from the hearth of mainstream American life. Representing gendered roles of family and workplace, an absence of racial difference, and worries about popular texts and consumerism, these mothers' letters argued for change in public policy governing the television programs their children viewed at home. They stand today as a repository of a set of American attitudes about media and society in the early fifties.

Framing public problems in terms of the family, these values of domestic responsibility also set much of the agenda for the broadcast reform movement of 1950–51. As they appealed for educational channels, broadcast reformers cast their arguments in the cultural grammar of the time, assuming a gendered, child-centered society in which TV was a private family matter. Like the mothers writing to Hennock, noncommercial broadcasters were homebound; they made the care of children their first priority. Emphasizing family ties, not progressive public speech, educational TV took its place in the ranch-style home of the fifties and settled in with an institutional mission that focused on the needs of middle-class children in school.

Constructing a Defensible, Coherent Argument: A Three-Pronged Petition for Instructional Channels

Although no educational broadcasters applied for television licenses prior to the FCC freeze on allocations in 1948, by late 1949 a movement had developed to seek as much as 20 percent of the spectrum for educational TV. Believing success was to be found in an articulate and tightly coordinated campaign, the broadcast reformers organized. They drafted materials, plotted central arguments, and cultivated the participation of prominent, well-spoken educators. Having worked for almost two years to construct eleven days of credible testimony, the JCET presented its case from November 27 to December 8, 1950. In total, seventy-six witnesses and 838 written statements from colleges, universities, school systems, and public service agencies were produced in support of nonprofit television's bid for the spectrum (Paulu 2).

Although Robert Blakely (1979: 15) reports that farmers, labor, and religious groups were represented, the hearings were dominated by educators and educational institutions. All referenced, in one way or another, the preferred position of education in American culture and television's potential for instruction. Clearly, for these educators what was at stake was the use of television to provide a broad-based, mainstream educational service for American schoolchildren and, to some extent, adults at home. These rhetors—teachers, school superintendents, education commissioners, and university presidents—did not speak for public media's loosely collected coalition of minority constituencies of the 1920s and 1930s. Rather, their discourse was framed within an invisible and unquestioned structure that presupposed noncommercial television to be educational.

Employing the rhetoric of the "electronic blackboard" and delineating themes of equal access, alternative service, and resource management, the broadcast reformers produced a three-pronged petition for reserved frequencies. They maintained first that educational broadcasting should have immediate access to the preferred and available technology of VHF, as well as UHF reservations for future develop-

ment. They further stated that the spectrum was a public resource subject to federal protection and that, as public domain, reserved frequencies were logically the preserve of public education. Finally, the
reformers claimed that the assumptions and practices of commercial
and noncommercial broadcasting made the two inherently different
and incapable of sustained collaboration, requiring dedicated channels
for educational broadcasting.

This was an old struggle with familiar arguments. The need for
spectrum, airwaves as public resources, and noncommercial broadcasting's alternative service were pivotal points in the broadcast reform movement of the mid-thirties. There were, however, important
differences in the fifties' fight for resources. As Ralph Engelman
(1996: 200) reports, the battle for the airwaves in 1934 had involved
a range of social and political interests, including educators, farmers,
labor, the church, and civil libertarians. Although generally situated
under the rubric of "educational radio," the broadcast reform movement was not exclusively academic or instructional but rather included a number of groups whose needs were not being met by commercial radio. These early broadcast reformers viewed their mission
as public; they sought to build a noncommercial media system that
addressed the material, intellectual, and cultural needs of their communities. Predicated on commitments to free speech and the claim
that the airwaves were a public good, these early broadcasters saw
radio as the cornerstone of progressive reform. They produced farm
extension programs in the Midwest; shows for the disadvantaged,
immigrant, and working classes of New York City; and series for the
labor community of Chicago. They broadcast political talk, local
performance, and historical dramas for schoolchildren. Importantly,
these broadcasters viewed their audiences as citizens, not consumers, and they were committed to enlarging the public sphere
through radio practice that gave voice to many levels of American
society. In a campaign that privileged educational TV as instructional technology, these interests, the underserved audiences they
represented, and their goals of broad social change largely evaporated.

Despite the narrow scope of reformers' strategy, their testimony provides a window on a complicated moment in U.S. television history,
when commercial profits began to climb and educators were increasingly denied access to facilities and airtime. These texts—transcripts of

witnesses' statements in the FCC proceedings—take us inside the hearing chambers. We hear the voices of teachers committed to their students, of a health educator knowledgeable about kinescopes and coaxial cable, and of an agricultural organizer who decries the disenfranchisement of rural audiences by networks seeking "quality" demographics in their listeners.[3]

VHF vs. UHF: Demanding Usable Spectrum Space

In 1950, educational broadcasters knew firsthand the problems associated with an undeveloped distribution technology, as the system's seventy-five FM stations aired radio programs most Americans could not hear.[5] Transmitting signals only one in five U.S. radios could receive at the time, educational broadcasters rightly worried that education's TV channels would be relegated to the similarly inaccessible and undeveloped UHF band. In October 1950, UHF broadcasting was wholly experimental. An October 9 memorandum from the NAEB notes that the only UHF television stations on the air were broadcasting transmission tests, and UHF receivers had yet to be developed and placed on the market (JCET allocations hearings). For the commercial station applicant, the UHF band offered no immediate income potential; prospects for noncommercial use seemed equally dim. Educational broadcasters feared UHF allocations would banish them to a zone of silence for a decade or more, as revealed in a memo of November 11, marked "urgent," from WFIU's manager Harold Skornia to Indiana University president H. B. Wells:

> Several proposals are before the Commission to save education space in the UHF. Here's the joker on this: To cover the same distance on UHF as covered by VHF requires several hundred times the power and investment. The RCA pilot UHF station in Bridgeport has never been able to reach more than three miles, with a fringe of up to seven miles, regardless of power. Tubes that will take high power at such tremendously high frequencies will always be very expensive and will be short-lived. They will not be available except experimentally, for what RCA estimates as 20 years (JCET allocations hearings).

Education's claims to immediate access of usable spectrum space were presented in general counsel Telford Taylor's opening arguments and repeated in virtually every statement thereafter. Noting that "all of the eight or nine million television receivers now in the hands of the public" were limited to VHF reception, Taylor requested that one VHF frequency be set aside for education in each metropolitan area and all major educational centers.[6] He also asked that 20 percent of the UHF band be allocated for noncommercial TV.

Calling on the commission to maintain a vision of the future as it allocated frequencies in the present, other witnesses also argued for education's right to immediate and long-term use of the spectrum. Following the lead of Howard Bevis, President of Ohio State University—who called for the reservation of educational channels for "keeps"—they maintained that those stations prepared to begin broadcasting immediately should be granted VHF allocations, while UHF frequencies should be held, on reserve, for future use. Education's case for frequencies necessarily hinged on arguments for accessible and exclusive spectrum space, long-term use, and nationwide coverage.

Public Domain: Conserving Frequencies for Education

The claim that the spectrum was public property emerged early in the course of the hearing. Ultimately, witnesses for noncommercial television would call on the rhetoric of conservation to construct a double argument for educational allocation of the spectrum. They maintained that the airwaves, though invisible, were a natural resource and subject to federal preservation; and that, as public domain, these reserved frequencies were logically and historically the preserve of public education. Belmont Farley cast the spectrum as a "peculiar property of the National Commonwealth" and called on the FCC to "secure the rights of education in the domain of the air." W. C. Toepelman of the American Council of Education likened the airwaves to public soils, mineral reserves, timber, and watersheds. Harriet Hester, representing the American Medical Association, argued that the radio spectrum was "provided by nature, . . . [was] in the category of natural resources, and as such [was] the property of all the people."

Historical precedent also figured in the reformers' arguments for dedicated spectrum for educational TV. Of special importance was the land-grant movement of the 1860s, which sought to make higher education a broad-based community resource through the practical arts and sciences. This tradition of public education, especially prominent in the Midwest, carried a philosophic legacy that placed public lands in the service of education, privileged home-based and rural constituencies, and stressed democratic participation. Educational broadcasting had strong ties to the land-grant tradition. Not only did early radio technology develop largely in the engineering laboratories of land-grant colleges and universities, these institutions were also among the first to operate AM stations. Even though many had been forced out of broadcasting by the early 1930s, Tracy Tyler (1933: 18) reports twenty-three land-grant institutions still owned noncommercial stations in 1933. All fulfilled broadcast commitments to extension and adult education, "reaching out," as Bevis argued, "to farms and homes to serve people where they lived." This practice, noted Michigan State president John Hannah, was consistent with an education movement characterized by commitments to "common people" and the "revolutionary notion that the work of universities should be closely related to the needs of the people" and available to all.

(Non)Commercial Broadcasting: A Discourse of Differentiation

Announcing its decision against dedicated AM frequencies on January 22, 1935, the FCC admonished educators and broadcasters to work together to discover the potential of educational broadcasting (Hill 1942: 71–72). Broadcast historians record this "partnership" as adversarial. As Eugene Leach writes, "Cooperation proved a hollow principle" (1983: 2). The incontrovertible differences between the premises, goals, and practices of commercial and noncommercial broadcasters surfaced again in educators' testimony at the hearings. Taylor noted that educational broadcasting stood on "an entirely different economic base" and produced programs "from an entirely distinct standpoint" than for-profit media. Noncommercial television's purpose, according to Bevis, was to "inform, enlighten, and instruct;" and Mark Schinnerer observed that its focus on public service distinguished it from stations and networks intent on attracting large audiences and selling airtime for profit. Even in this discourse of differentiation, however, the educators made efforts to contain the potentially accusatory and acrimonious critique of an old adversary. As Taylor noted,

> Our purpose here is not to excuse past failures [by educators] or level the finger of criticism at the commercial broadcasting industry. We recognize that the commercial broadcasters have their own difficult problems to solve, and if some decisions that have been made now appear unwise or shortsighted, nevertheless human fallibility is not peculiar to the radio industry.

Subsequent testimony was sprinkled with phrases of conciliation and praise: "we recognize the right of free enterprise to employ national resources in the economic interest of this nation," said Farley; "no one can deny the advantages which commercial broadcasting has given us," Hester added; Hull pointed to "valuable (though sporadic) activity on the part of commercial stations and networks in public service broadcasting." Park Livingston, a Trustee of the University of Illinois predicted optimistically that stations, "publicly owned, [can] operate side by side with private stations without friction."

Despite the uneasy civility of these statements, the record itself is a less compromising witness, revealing an increasing unwillingness by commercial broadcasting to cooperate with noncommercial entities. As television developed into a profitable venture, stations and networks were allocating fewer production resources and less airtime to noncommercial projects. James Marshall, for example, reported that the New York City schools had produced sixty-five television programs in the years 1945–47, but

> in the past three years [1948–50], our opportunities for cooperation with the local commercial stations have been almost non-existent. . . . Not a single program of all those planned was ever broadcast. Although interest in educational programming is very frequently expressed at the networks, the exigencies of budget and commercial scheduling completely nullify these good intentions. Clearly, the schools cannot count on adequate help or time allotment from networks whose primary purpose must be to sell time to advertisers.

Robert Engler, legislative secretary of the National Farmers' Union, maintained broadcasting's potential to enhance farm life had been dissipated by commercial radio's disregard for rural audiences:

> We have long been aware of the tremendous potentialities of radio for better farm living and for diminishing the isolation of agricultural life. . . . Unfortunately, farmers and their families have discovered that the promise of radio has generally been greater than its actual performance. . . .
> Farm people in all sections of the country have seen how radio stations in their communities have given inadequate time to matters of farm and local interest; how farm programs have had their schedules changed frequently and are often presented at times which are inconvenient for those who work on the farms. Worthwhile network

programs like the "National Farm and Home Hour" have been chipped away at until their original purposes have been lost. . . .

The big powerful metropolitan stations simply do not give farm people and others the public services which their special needs require.

Constance Warren, representing the American Association of University Women, found commercial stations reluctant to "release enough or appropriate time" from their paid programs to support education:

Our experience is that radio has over the years devoted less and less time to educational programs. . . . Our members have often been disappointed about the presentation of good educational programs because the radio stations were not willing to give them time. An example in point is in Little Rock, Arkansas, where for three years the AAUW branch had been denied the opportunity to present a fine program called "The Kindergarten of the Air."

And finally, Hester reported the only time available for kinescoping an American Medical Association production was between midnight and 7 a.m.; crews secured for the job were paid overtime. She recalled attempts to produce new programs:

Only recently, the Bureau of Health Education offered to provide a half-hour dramatic script on problems of doctor supply in small communities, written by a topflight author. We offered to pay all talent costs, including Walter Hampden as lead. We would supply our own producer, all props, and all sets beyond the materials available in the studio.

We did not ask for coaxial cable, but offered to purchase kinescopes for circulation to other stations throughout the country, giving first refusal in each community to the station affiliated with that network.

Since the script held elements which might later be expanded into a successful commercial series which could be sold with A.M.A. endorsement to acceptable sponsors, we offered that station and network first refusal on any such future possibility.

We were refused.

In all cases, educators worried that the trend in television would follow those of commercial radio—refusing production services, cluttering content with advertising breaks, and pushing nonprofit programs to the margins of the broadcast day when few listeners were available. Earl McGrath, a Commissioner for the U.S. Office of Education, reported that educators found it impossible to get regular recurring broadcast time at hours most suitable for educational use, while Engler said that some were being "squeezed out entirely by bids from high-powered and well-financed soap companies for desirable and expensive radio time." The Protestant Radio Commission's Clayton Griswold observed that "no commercial television station is attempting to do anything like an adequate job in the field of education." In the face of this grim reality, Marshall's questions for the future were ominous: "If this is true today in the early stages of television, what chance is there for education on commercial stations as sponsored programs increase in number and greater competition intensifies the battle for favorable time on the air?"

The reformers agreed unanimously that the solution lay in reserved channels for noncommercial broadcasting. New York City's director of radio, Seymour Siegel, spoke for all nonprofit broadcasters when he said, "The City needs its own television station."

In 1950, as educators argued for public resource management, they swam upstream against dominant ideology that privileged a socially responsible private sector working in the public interest. Although their claim that the airwaves were public property was consistent with the discourse of spectrum allocation, the inherent bias of long-term practice negated the power of this argument. It is not surprising, then, that the reformers' case for public resources and public interest was challenged by members of the FCC and commercial broadcasting during the allocation hearings. Blakely quotes FCC commissioner Rosel Hyde to the effect that the radio spectrum should not be considered a limited public resource. While some natural resources could be depleted, Hyde said, "the radio frequencies continue on for use regardless of what immediate use might be made of them. . . . Hence the opportunity for the educator is always open, you might say." Citing the FCC decision against set-aside frequencies on the AM band and the fact that no new noncommercial AM stations had gone on the air since the 1935 ruling, educational broadcasters argued that the commercial allocation of a channel closed education's opportunity for that frequency as effectively as the physical depletion of a resource (Blakely 1979: 17).

Frank Stanton, president of Columbia Broadcasting System, argued that the public interest would actually be damaged by nationwide reservations for noncommercial educational use. Testifying before the FCC on January 25, 1951, Stanton maintained that a "rounded service for the majority of families" should take precedence over a "special television service for a minority of the community. . . . The first consideration must be a service which appeals to most of the people most of the time" (JCET allocations hearings). Stanton testified that widespread reservation of channels for education would jeopardize a competitive, general television service and its ability to attract a "mass audience." Stanton's testimony did not overtly disparage the concept of educational programming: "We are all agreed, I am sure, that television is a great medium and that education is a great force for good." His strategy, rather, was twofold: first, to discount the ability of educators to develop successful stations—"There must also be weighed the fact that the history of educational use of AM certainly furnishes the basis for reasonable doubts as to whether, even with blanket reservation, there ever will be a significant number of noncommercial educational stations"—and, secondly, to argue for a competitive, city-by-city review of noncommercial applications: "We are convinced that the recommended approach of a case-by-case method of deciding these problems. . . holds far greater promise of best serving the public interest than would an inflexible across-the-board formula which must necessarily ignore the variables in each community situation." It seems the prime objective of Stanton's testimony was to persuade FCC commissioners that America's public interest was equated with the market's interest, and that both were best served by a strong commercial television system and the programming it offered to a large mainstream audience. To this end, he opposed action that would remove any portion of the spectrum from commercial access, splinter the developing U.S. television audience, or establish the structure for a new network. Unlike that of most educators, Stanton's testimony did not address issues of resource protection. An "educational band" for television was viewed not as a domain preserved for public use, but as a competitive incursion into a zone developed and controlled by commercial broadcasters for profit activity. If the educators' arguments retraced old ground, so too did Stanton's. Significantly, his efforts to protect the networks' broad-based audience cohered with the FCC admonition in 1934 that the "mass medium performs most properly when it reaches the broadest, 'most mass' audience possible" (qtd. in J. Brown 1989: 279).

Perhaps most striking, however, was the lack of commercial response to the reformers' hearing. The broadcast reformers took the 1950–51 hearings seriously. Remembering the movement's lack of planning, organization, and coherent argument in the allocation hearings of 1934, they determined to mount a credible campaign for television frequencies. As a result, the educators produced eleven days of testimony, which included 76 witnesses, 838 written statements, and 64 exhibits. In sharp contrast, the industry's presentation was far less substantial (with five witnesses and six exhibits) and hastily prepared (Blakely 1979: 4). As *Broadcasting*, the leading trade journal, reported in January 1951:

> Almost too late organized radio and TV will seek to balance the record on the demands of organized educators who would have Uncle Sam reserve at least 20 percent of available TV spectrum space for pure, unadorned education. Until quite recently there have been no comers from the commercial side of TV (qtd. in Blakely 1979: 20).

That the NAB and commercial networks did not deem it necessary to mount a full and compelling defense before the FCC suggests that industry leaders expected, from the outset, an allocation ruling favoring commercial interests.

11.7 Percent of the Spectrum: A Hollow Victory

On April 14, 1952, the Federal Communications Commission (FCC) announced 2,053 new TV assignments for the U.S. and its territories. Of these, 242 (233 in the continental United States and nine for territories) were reserved for education. The long-awaited Sixth Order and Report allocated 162 UHF and 71 VHF noncommercial frequencies for the continental U.S. and decreed that noncommercial television would be strictly educational and nonprofit. In all, noncommercial broadcasters were awarded 11.7 percent of the spectrum (Paulu n.d.: 6). The popular press was jubilant: "Along with the robins and crocuses has come the unfreezing of the television industry. . . . The decision by the FCC to set aside channels for educational interests in 242 communities is most heartening. . . . The possibilities for educational TV are enormous and breath-taking!" (JCET n.d.: 1). Broadcast reformers, however, rightly perceived the FCC allocation ruling as a hollow victory. Not only did the allotment fall significantly short of the movement's goal of 20 percent, but most of the allocations for education were located in the still unavailable domain of UHF. Even more damaging, fully one fourth of the country's metropolitan centers were given no reservations at all (Paulu n.d.: 6). In practical terms, this meant that most Americans would wait a decade or more before noncommercial stations developed in their communities.

Most problematic, however, was the narrow scope of noncommercial TV's largely self-defined service and sphere of influence. The visual trope of "electronic blackboard" would stunt the growth of noncommercial broadcasting, defining noncommercial television as a teaching tool. A static image woven into traditional pedagogy, the blackboard metaphor positioned educational TV in the classroom, not the neighborhood, and privileged the speech of teachers instead of students. Speaking in 1949 at the Allerton House seminars, Paul Lazarsfeld had worried that the myopia of educational broadcasters might prevent their seeing the public potential of television: "I am also afraid that it will not be quite so easy for you to realize what we are talking about—what we want from you—because there is a danger that you educators will have a hard time in detaching yourselves from the classroom situation" (Lazarsfeld 1949).

His fears would seem justified. Martin Maloney, writing eighteen years later, noted the central questions of educational television historically had been technical and pedagogical: "Can we teach by television, who learns best by television, and how do teachers feel about teaching by television?" (1969: 15). These issues guided the work of Philip Lewis, who claimed educational TV's best use was in "partially relieving the classroom teacher from routine preparation and delivery of expository material, thus leaving her free to concentrate on the individual needs of the student" (1961: 31). They also framed Wilbur Schramm's questions in 1962 about television's potential in the classroom:

> The spectrum of instructional uses of television is not completely known. It is clear that there are some teaching acts it can do superlatively well. It can let a large number of students look into a microscope at the same time, or watch surgical procedures from close at hand. It can let a class watch an activity that would be spoiled by direct observation. (4)

Schramm's vision of educational TV—the performance of "teaching acts"—is revealed here as one of spectators, not actors; it did not reflect the vision of a robust public participating in socially responsible discourse for the good of the community. The practical lessons of citizenship, touching on themes of diversity, social change, and democracy, did not extend into the realm of "teaching television."

This narrow definition of purpose developed partly as a response to the social and political moment in which noncommercial TV was introduced. The move to construct a child-centered, largely depoliticized public media service would seem a logical compromise for noncommercial broadcasting in the early 1950s, as broadcast reformers, working within the cultural constraints of homebound domesticity and the chilling political climate of McCarthyism, produced an "acceptable discourse" about public channels. Elisabeth Noelle-Neumann (1974: 44) writes that public opinion—necessarily a "matter of speaking and of silence"—arises from an interaction of people with their social environments. Fearing social isolation, sanction, and outright punishment, individuals select and voice the viewpoints they perceive as dominant. The more this happens, as one opinion is heard more frequently and more confidently, secondary views are correspondingly voiced less and less. This interactive process sets in motion a spiral by which given attitudes prevail and establish public norms.

Taking their cues from the restrictive postwar culture of the time and remembering spectrum losses of the past, noncommercial broadcasters made deliberate choices of speaker and topic that worked to narrow the debate over frequencies. The battle for radio channels in 1934, although largely disorganized, had nonetheless represented a range of constituencies and experiences, with significant contributions from labor, organized religion, the left, education, agriculture, and amateurs. A similarly rich resource base for noncommercial TV was demonstrated by the coalition of educators, parents, club women, extension specialists, and labor and religious leaders that started Alabama Educational Television in 1953 ("12 Groups Join Forces" 1953).[7] Testimony at the FCC hearings on broadcast editorializing in February 1948 was also mixed. Groups as varied as the United Automobile Workers, Chicago Federation of Labor, American Jewish Congress, Cornell University, Revere Racing Association, Farmers Union of America, Institute for Education by Radio, Radio Writers Guild, Joint Religious Radio Committee, Iowa Association of Radio News Editors, and the three commercial networks offered comments (JCET allocations hearings).

Despite this broad-based interest in radio and television, the dominant voice heard in the frequency hearings was that of mainstream education. In producing a coherent argument for noncommercial frequencies, the JCET had erased the talk of difference, so that in 1950–51—amid the national debate on "separate but equal" schooling—there was no discussion in the FCC hearings of how noncommercial TV could usefully impact the lives of black children being schooled in lesser and segregated facilities. Although the Association of Negro Land-Grant Colleges had been active for decades, this organization was not called as a witness for the land-grant tradition. Further, on November 3, 1950, a memo by NAEB president Richard Hull purged remaining voices from the margin:

> Item 17: DO NOT USE [civil rights advocate Clifford] DURR. And probably not Patton [of the National Farmers' Union] either. . . .
> Item 21: RE AUGUSTANA SYNOD—IF THIS GETS DIRTY ENUF WE CAN BRING IN RELIGIOUS GROUPS. AS OF NOW MY ADVICE IS NO. . . .
> Item 23: Regarding Baptist and Methodist Representatives— Depends on DIRTY and 21 above (JCET allocations hearings).[8]

This memo, excising representatives of religion, agriculture, and the left from the agenda, stands as striking evidence of noncommercial broadcasting's move to delimit the rhetorical range of its argument. Not everyone was granted the floor, and as speakers were strategically silenced, so were the communities and viewpoints they represented. What remained was a claim for the status quo and the designation of noncommercial broadcasting as a tool for a traditional pedagogical style.

Finally, the perspectives and future service of educational broadcasting were narrowed by the discourse it produced and the audience it constructed through that discourse at the FCC hearings. Noncommercial broadcasters, promoting a white, middle-class educational TV service, delivered an argument that they considered properly persuasive for their audience of FCC commissioners. By inferring an audience that privileged the status quo, they constructed one (E. Black 1970: 110). This resulted in an even more powerful ideology of educational broadcasting, defining and (re)defining assumptions about the terms and obligations of noncommercial TV. The hearing discourse created a dominant public opinion that would overshadow all other arguments about the course of noncommercial television. James Day (1995: 23–25) writes that the noncommercial broadcasting community of the fifties was not of one mind about the educational definitions of public media, noting that some "envisioned a broader mission." Even so, a view of public TV as educational would emerge as the dominant public opinion. Through the continued articulation of a pedagogic vision at the expense of arguments for a public mission, public media came to be defined "naturally" as educational. The campaign that broadcast reformers waged for a presence on the spectrum, working within their own needs for success and worries about formal and informal sanction, silenced discussions of publicness and television. As these broadcasters consciously selected some rhetorical stances and speakers over others, they cultivated a persuasive environment that allowed the educational mission to dominate the conversation, to gain allegiance from a range of groups, and finally to become entrenched as the public's opinion.

The process by which alternative definitions of public media were silenced is further illustrated by dialogue from a Senate Interstate Commerce Committee hearing on July 18, 1951. FCC commissioner Wayne Coy called up, as his own concepts, those arguments presented by the educators seven months earlier:

> **Sen. O'Connor:** What is considered an educational program?
> **Commissioner Coy:** An educational program today is one that is put on by an educational institution and has to do with the improvement of cultural background and understanding. An example of such a program is. . .
> **Sen. Benton:** University of Chicago Round Table!
> **Sen. Capehart:** American Forum of the Air!
> **Commissioner Coy:** No. An example of an educational program is a program put on by the University of Michigan over a television station in Detroit having to do with various subjects in the curriculum of the University of Michigan (JCET allocations hearings).

Even as Benton and Capehart sought to push educational programming into the public arena, Coy confined it to the classroom, reiterating the dominant opinion promulgated by reformers that noncommercial TV had an in-school mission. This is not to suggest that the FCC was not initially inclined toward a view of noncommercial TV as a safe and sanitized teaching tool. Very likely, broadcast reformers were accurate in assessing the commissioners as more sympathetic to an "educational" frame than a "public" one. Even so, their decision to exploit this as a means of achieving space on the spectrum would prove shortsighted, as it institutionalized a limited conception of noncommercial television in the minds of reformers, educators, and the general public. Through construction of the most defensible argument, reformers forfeited an opportunity to drive the discussion into a larger, more contested rhetorical terrain. Such discourse could have enabled a bold public initiative in the fifties; it would most certainly have sustained what broadcast reformer Dick Hull called a "social dream" for future generations.

Education as Social Reform: Lessons from Dewey

A perusal of the PBS web page, as well as any evening's program schedule, reveals the paucity of public-spirited, noncommercial, and truly alternative fare on public TV. There is little evidence of commitments to change, social reform, or the interactive and useful public spaces discussed by James Curran, Douglas Kellner, and John Peters. Calling itself a "safe harbor" for children, public broadcasting is actually a tame and risk-aversive institution that sidesteps controversy as easily as it offers a how-to show on Saturday afternoon. Especially troubling is the reluctance of public broadcasters to apply the lessons of progressives such as John Dewey to solve social problems, develop innovative teaching, and create public spaces for dialogue. Dewey maintained that education was a process of social life and the means for social change. Education is not only the necessary precondition for societal reform, but actually the foundation of democratic practice. Dewey advocated experiential engagement and the "busy workshop," and was adamantly opposed to top-down teaching and passive reception (Dewey 1900: 48, 91). Dewey's was a pedagogy of social life and classroom activity, a theory with commitments to daily life, neighborly ties, and interactive students, teachers, and texts. His work stands today, as it did in 1900 and 1950–51, as a standard for innovative, student-based education.

Public TV's efforts in education are also widely and rightly acclaimed. On average, U.S. public stations air five and one-half hours of instructional broadcasting every day, with 24 million American schoolchildren receiving some part of their curriculum from television and video. Since its introduction in 1950–51, educational TV has become an indispensable player in the American classroom:

> Public television's instructional programming has been popular with teachers from the beginning because almost all of it is custom-made and curriculum-driven. Accompanied by printed teaching materials and other aids, much of it is of high quality. . . . Nor is there a lack of quantity; in the summer of 1992, more than 120 new instructional series were available to schools for the first time. As a producer of instructional programming, the public television community has no peer (*Twentieth Century Fund* 1993: 24).

As innovative and successful as these programs are, most of them are clearly instructional materials, not interactive lessons for living. Described by the Twentieth Century Fund task force as "aids to education," "tools for teachers," and "technologies in the classroom," they are a contemporary version of the top-down, ready-made, teacher-directed materials Dewey opposed. A student, Dewey reminds us, should not be "one who stands at the end of a pipe line receiving material conducted from a distant reservoir of learning" (1931: 34). Whether the reservoir is the superintendent's office, the local university, or PBS, the result is the same: programs built for "listening."

Further, lacking a reform agenda, educational television offers materials that serve teacher lesson plans, not democratic process and community life. In the years since 1950–51, the system's internalized sense of confidence and purpose has been crippled. Thus public broadcasting has failed to promote Dewey's vision of schools as enablers of democratic practice and social reform: "I believe education is the fundamental method of social progress and reform. I believe that all reforms which rest simply upon changes in mechanical or outward arrangements are transitory and futile" (qtd. in Kloppenberg 1986: 374).

Despite public broadcasting practice that prescribes in-school TV as largely illustrative and classroom-bound, models do exist for Dewey-like approaches to educational television. Just as the terms "engaging," "interactive," and "experiential" invoke Dewey's theory of education, they also describe film producer Steven Spielberg's StarBright World, Project IMPACT, and Breakthrough to Literacy, an innovative early reading program developed at the University of Iowa. StarBright World is an interactive, in-hospital computer network that allows seriously ill children from across the nation to interact with one another. Engaging in educational activities and conversation, they help each other cope with the day-to-day realities of illness: loneliness, pain, fear, and depression. Project IMPACT was developed by the Los Angeles County public school system as a way to provide quality science instruction in urban and rural elementary schools through video lessons and student-driven experiments. In order to utilize the materials, however, teachers frequently find they must readjust their teaching styles, developing new strategies that enable student voices and participation (Powell 1997).

The interactive software program Breakthrough to Literacy was designed on the premise that each child learns to read differently; it allows children to master early reading skills from their own computer work stations. The project has proved especially successful with children from at-risk environments, who often encounter challenging home situations and life experiences that define them as failures even before they enter kindergarten (Brown 1998). Each of these projects brings individualized, interactive, and student-driven approaches to mediated lessons. Importantly, each also addresses serious social issues, from retraining teachers to granting children important conversations and new definitions of self-worth. Employing new technologies and exploring bold concepts, each strives to make a difference in the lives of children.

Similarly, the Hubert H. Humphrey Institute of Public Affairs at the University of Minnesota and the California Center for Civic Participation not only encourage young people to become involved in the democratic process, but teach them how to do it. PBS could partner effectively with such organizations, pursuing projects to help children and teens develop skills in critical thinking, democratic discourse, and community leadership. A hypothetical project might find broadcasters working in collaboration with the California Center to advance high school students' knowledge of water policy. Public broadcasters could produce video segments and accompanying printed materials dealing with the history and practices of water use in California. These materials could be distributed to the state's high schools, and policy experts, fishermen, historians, politicians, and lawyers would be summoned to present their views and answer students' questions through an interactive broadcasting format. Students would be encouraged to develop their own texts—radio and television programs, CDs, web pages, and public speeches—about water policy. They would debate the issues with one another in class. On a given day, all participating students from throughout the state could convene in a free discursive space comprised of an interactive chat room, television studio, phone lines, and Instructional Television Fixed Service (ITFS) studio facilities. The resulting conversation would be facilitated, not by a teacher, but by student peers trained in group discussion. The objective would be a recommendation on water policy, written by high school students and presented to the California state legislature. Students would be encouraged to attend and participate in legislative hearings and committee meetings. This hands-on, experiential engagement with public work could result in confidence, knowledge of policy making, expertise in political discourse, and a desire to participate in democratic process. Education, in this scenario, becomes an instrument of citizenship and community.

Though the human and technological resources required for such a program are far from prohibitive, projects of this kind are rare to nonexistent on public television. Instead of developing "busy workshops" for students, station instructional TV directors are more often seen hawking their products as "best buys" in the educational marketplace. The following announcement appeared consistently throughout the latter half of the 1990s on the KERA/Dallas educational services web page (www.kera.org/erc/erecteach.html):

Attention Teachers—The KERA/KDTN Educational Resource Center (ERC) has worked with teachers and administrators throughout North Texas for more than 35 years. We offer member school districts nearly 2,000 hours of curriculum-based instructional programs for only $1.50 per student. This fee includes printed support materials, correlations with TAAS [Texas Assessment of Academic Skills] and essential elements, broadcast schedules and on-site workshops. It is THE most economical educational programming service around.

Ultimately, the case for frequencies in 1950–51 was a strategic compromise that has cost public broadcasting not only its institutional identity but also a world view. The compromises made almost fifty years ago, as noncommercial broadcasters sought a concept they could sell to a latently hostile FCC, curtailed the system's public mission. Today, without a core self-definition and decades-long history of pub-licness, public television lacks the creative energy and self-confidence to move meaningfully in the daily lives of many American people.

In 1949, Allerton House participants discussed what the fledgling noncommercial television service should be called. The Rockefeller Foundation's John Marshall wrote to Wilbur Schramm on February 6, 1950:

> I still wonder if it is wise to set this work up under the head of "educa-tional broadcasting." The people in the non-commercial stations as I see it are simply trying to do something else which, to be sure, turns out to be educational, serious, and I believe considerably more satisfying to the very large group of people in this country who now simply don't lis-ten. What we should all like to see tried, I believe, is ways in which broadcasting can do some of the things that it is not now doing. . . . For example, is the traditional phrase, public service broadcasting, out of the question? (Rockefeller Foundation Papers)

From the outset, U.S. noncommercial broadcasters have faced much ad-versity, including a laissez-faire broadcasting system; lack of funding and spectrum resources; and powerful industry, regulatory, and political op-position. In the 1950s, broadcast reformers could have conceivably em-ployed educational broadcasting as a sensible strategy for surmounting those obstacles. The social currency of educational television could have made it an important wedge for noncommercial broadcasters in efforts to gain ground for broader applications of public service broadcasting. Un-fortunately, such a project required foundational resources absent in nonprofit broadcasting's organizational culture. Lacking deep commit-ments to an active, multidimensional, and responsive public sphere, noncommercial broadcasters could not expand beyond the classroom.

In the end, the name—and the limitations—of educational broad-casting stuck.

Notes

Portions of this chapter previously appeared in "Domestic Values and Na-tional Security: Framing the Battle for Educational Frequencies in 1950–51," *Journal of Communication Inquiry* 25:4 (October 2001), 414–437. © 2001 by Sage Publications. Reprinted by permission of Sage Publications.

1. Facing a dead end with the FCC, the Paulists contacted the White House early in 1936 in hopes of "regaining those facilities WLWL enjoyed prior to 1928 when without a legal hearing, or even advance notice, [the station] was drastically curtailed under most questionable circumstances" (Early 1936). Despite appeals to the White House and the FCC from many (including the archbishop of New York; the bishops of Brooklyn, Newark, Trenton, and Hartford dioceses; the president of the International Catholic Truth Society; and the governor of New York) Roosevelt made it clear he would not support the Paulists' claims to the spectrum.

In 1937, WLWL sold to Arde Bulova, the watch manufacturer, for $275,000 (McChesney 1993: 228).

2. In 1949–50, the median age for marrying dropped to twenty years, three months for women and to twenty-two years, seven months for men. The birthrate climbed from eighteen births per thousand in 1937 to twenty-eight per thousand in 1947 and twenty-five per thousand in 1950. The marriage rate for unmarried American females exceeded 85 percent in 1950; and marriages forged in the late 1940s proved to be especially stable, holding the divorce rate below projections through the mid-sixties (E. May 1988: 6–8).

3. Information and quotations on the following pages are taken from the witness statements of Howard L. Bevis, Robert Engler, Belmont Farley, Clayton Griswold, John Hannah, Harriet Hester, Richard Hull, Ira Jarrell, Park Livingston, James Marshall, Earl McGrath, Mark Schinnerer, Seymour Siegel, Telford Taylor, W. C. Toepelman, and Constance Warren. The statements and other materials related to the hearings are held in the Ohio State University archives.

4. The danger extended throughout American society. Among the many victims were Eugene William Landy, who was refused a commission in the Naval Reserve because his mother had once been a Communist (Stone 1963: 85); Annie Lee Moss, an elderly black woman accused of Communist party membership through confusion with another woman of the same name (Stone 1963: 30); and Dr. George Stoddard, who was forced to resign as president of the University of Illinois for laxness in hunting down Communists on the Illinois faculty (Diamond 1992: 265).

5. FM reception problems surfaced in correspondence from Hull to Edwin C. Johnson, chair of the Senate Interstate Commerce Committee, on June 19, 1950, when Hull sought help in requiring TV receiver manufacturers to include FM tuners in their sets. Hull also took the opportunity to report that the U.S. Bureau of the Census, "despite pressure from all sides," had refused to include an FM ownership question in recent census tabulation (Hull 1950). Hull claimed FM reception dilemmas were not technical but were due instead to social and economic forces that required FM to make a "second start" after reallocation of the FM band in 1945 and then placed it in the shadow of a

more glamorous televisual medium in the late forties. Further, said Hull, in addition to failed listener and advertiser support caused by limited circulation of FM receivers, most FM licensees were also AM licensees who applied for FM stations as a "hedge" and hence took a "wait and see" attitude instead of pushing the new medium, and in some cases, apparently took "anti-FM measures" (Hull 1950).

6. Taylor defined a "metropolitan center" as at least one city with a population of 50,000 or more and contiguous counties closely integrated with the city. The term major educational center was intended to cover small communities outside metropolitan areas in which a large educational institution—typically with an enrollment of at least 5,000—was located (Taylor 3).

7. Sponsors included the University of Alabama Extension Center, Howard College, Birmingham-Southern College, the Jefferson County Radio and Television Council, the Birmingham Industrial Union Council–United Mine Workers, the Alabama Federation of Women's Clubs, the Jefferson County Council of Public School Superintendents, the Classroom Teachers Association, the Jefferson County Council of Parents and Teachers, the Junior League of Birmingham, and the Birmingham Branch of the National Council of Christians and Jews ("12 Groups Join Forces").

8. Durr was a controversial and outspoken advocate of civil rights and free speech who openly opposed J. Edgar Hoover's investigations of Americans "suspected of possible pro-Russian activity." A Roosevelt appointee to the FCC who was instrumental in having FM channels set aside for noncommercial use, he served on the commission for seven years and ultimately resigned his seat rather than take Truman's loyalty oath (Durr 1947). He and his wife Virginia were investigated by the HUAC for their civil rights work in the South and forced to defend themselves in open hearings in New Orleans in 1954. They were found innocent. They counted a number of public broadcasters among their friends, including Dallas Smythe (Institute of Communications Research, University of Illinois), Frank Schooley (WILL/Urbana), Telford Taylor (JCET general counsel), Graydon Ausmus (Alabama ETV), Harold McCarty (WHA/Wisconsin), Tracy Tyler (NCER), and Keith Tyler (WOSU/Columbus).

CHAPTER FOUR

Community and Performance: Getting the Whole Town Talking

Director: Hello, Norm. This is Master Control. We'll take Runnells in Monitor Four.

[Norm Bernhauer]: Waiting for cue.

Director: Go ahead.

N.B.: This is Norm Bernhauer, and you're going down the main street of Runnells, twelve miles east of Des Moines in central Iowa. Population: three hundred seven. In Runnells, the whole town's talking!

Dwight Hunnel says, "Let's face it. Either we build a new water system or this town's dead."

Mrs. Viola Welshaur says, "Other towns have decent water. Why doesn't Runnells?"

But for H.O. Tuttle, the issue is what good is a water system if the town goes bankrupt building it.

May 1st, 1952! To Runnells, Iowa, the town with a problem, comes television, to catch the face and the voice of America itself!

(MUSIC UP)

—*The Whole Town's Talking*, May 1, 1952

The Whole Town's Talking was an experiment in democratic discourse. Funded by the Ford Foundation and produced and aired by WOI-TV in Ames, Iowa, this fifteen-part television series aimed to get the citizens of Iowa talking about issues of common concern. In the case of Runnells, the topic was a new water system. Residents of Cambridge, Eldora, Story City, and Winterset discussed education; parents met in Toledo to talk about teen recreation; citizens in Guthrie sought ways to replace their worn-out courthouse. On April 17, 1952, thirty representatives of the Sac and Fox tribal councils met to discuss the need for more land and better homes, how to keep their own schools, and the problems of cultural assimilation for their children (Hartzell, Smith, and Bernanek n.d.: 29–33).

In each instance, *The Whole Town's Talking* was an effort to instigate vigorous discussion and broad-based citizen participation in community life. Overtly local, political, and grassroots in its orientation, this earliest example of national public television programming provided protected, public space for democratic talk about common problems. Seeking to use television performance as the springboard for organized community action, *The Whole Town's Talking* set out to prove that the residents of Iowa could face, discuss, and ultimately solve the real problems of their towns. In Runnells, the dilemma was the lack of a central water system. Only two businesses had running water; a number of homes did not. Many residents carried water by the bucketful every day to provide safe drinking water for their families. Three times a bond issue for the water system was put to a vote; three times it failed to carry. Yet a portion of this town of 307 believed adequate water could save their community. They decided to vote again. WOI's decision to explore this existing community controversy formed the basis of the last episode of *The Whole Town's Talking*. Gathering a number of people together in the basement of the First Christian Church on May 1, 1952, the show opened its microphone to a range of opinions about the use of common resources. What resulted was anger, hostility, conciliation, a measure of consensus, and the largest turnout ever at the polls four days later. The voices heard that night were not those of elites; all citizens had equal access to the floor. Like other segments of the series that granted public speech to Indian children, housewives, farmers, businesspeople, and local politicians, the voices heard in Runnells' church basement were the talk of the town.

The Runnells episode of *The Whole Town's Talking* opened with a shot of the control room. The camera panned past the assistant director, four television monitors, and the switcher. Never slowing, the shot zoomed into a fifth monitor, moving past and into the title "Runnells,

Iowa" to a sweeping panorama of the town's Main Street. Only then did the content focus on the people and the problem of Runnells. Framed explicitly within the technology of television, *The Whole Town's Talking* was more than a series about towns with problems. Itself a part of the discursive process, TV became speaker, spectator, and cocreator of meaning in a collaborative exploration of the common good. Cameras, cables, and technical crew were inserted into the text, as the series sought ways to enable democratic practice through a spontaneous, interactive, and performative use of mass media. In blurring the lines between television and televised, this TV Town Hall became a piece of the neighborhood.

"Runnells, Iowa" closed as the director swiveled to gaze into the camera. Removing his headset, he made an impassioned direct address to the television audience:

> My name is Charles Guggenheim, and I'm the director and producer of *The Whole Town's Talking* series, which ends this evening. The title of director and producer is sort of misleading, because not one man produces and directs a show like this. The names of some of the people you see every evening when the show is on are on the titles at the end of the program. But there are many more. There are the floor director, the cameramen, the film technicians, the audio technicians, and the production assistant. They too deserve credit for the production and direction of this series.
>
> But more important than the people outside the show are the people inside the show—the housewives, the merchants, the Iowa farmer who has had the integrity to come on this program and to stand up on his own feet and say what he believes. These are the real heroes of this production and without them, this series could never have been made possible.
>
> And now, through the miracle of television film, people all over the country and later people all over the world will see the Iowa people get up on their feet and prove that grassroots democracy can still live in a vital manner!
> (REPLACE HEADSET.)
> OK, Burnie, pan right. Ready to super four. Super four. Music.
> (MUSIC UP.)

Exploring the intersections of technology, community, and democracy, *The Whole Town's Talking* was educational television's first national series.

As a modern-day polis, the show demonstrated television's great potential to build a problem-solving and participatory community through engaged civic talk. Not only did the series get the towns of Iowa talking, it also got them acting. Tangible results of the "town talks" initiated by *The Whole Town's Talking* included a campaign to revitalize the Cambridge High School, a vote in Slager to de-emphasize high school athletics, formation of a Rainbow Girls organization in Toledo, and a central water system in Runnells (Hartzell, Smith, and Bernanek n.d.: 29–33).

The series was nothing short of revolutionary. Unfortunately, it was also one of a kind. Public broadcasting's significant promise in community-building was cut short in the 1960s by the system's lack of sustained commitment to neighborhood discourses and grassroots democracy. Two major factors worked to alter the community-centered institutional character of public television, robbing it of a foundation in bottom-up governance, local debate, and popular expertise. The first was the social moment in which the Public Television Act was introduced. Promoted by Lyndon Johnson as a tool of enlightenment, public TV reflected the centrist liberalism and top-down federalism of his administration. Like many other pieces of the Great Society, public TV functioned as a paternalistic movement that cast elites as authorities and typically avoided alliances with grassroots constituencies. Further, public TV's late entrance put it before the American people in a moment of social upheaval and presidential decline. Introduced on the crest of the sixties' social movements and voted into law on the eve of 1968, the Public Television Act was subsumed by events that would mark the beginning of a conservative ascendancy in the U.S. Importantly, the public TV bill also missed the 1964–66 window of Great Society social reform, partnering public broadcasting with more peripheral efforts to enhance the humanities in the U.S. Public broadcasting's failure to align itself with movements tied to fundamental social change kept the new system at the edges of American social life.

Just as the Great Society contained public TV's potential as a change agent, the Ford Foundation's influence limited its range, scope, and audience base. Moving through a liberal arts initiative into public policy and taste engineering, the foundation put educational TV to use in meeting its own agenda for U.S. society: promoting liberal arts education, elite culture, and governance by experts. Not only did this work to authorize the discourse and interests of the educated classes, it also contained diversity, silenced popular speech, and entrenched a class-based hierarchy of knowledge and taste.

Framed by the high federalism of LBJ's Great Society and the social and cultural agenda of the Ford Foundation, public TV abandoned its early roots in local performance to become not an advocate for community, but rather an expert, a distanced and paternalistic authority. The impacts of this shift from educational broadcasting's original purposes have been significant. A primary source of America's "quality" TV, public television not only acts as benevolent teacher (positioning its audience as passive) but has evolved to become a social regulator that reinforces norms and class differentiations. With this change in institutional focus, the goals of the system's first national series—to employ television technology in inventing an interactive, community-based public sphere—have largely evaporated.

Democratic Media: Limitations of the Great Society

Although *The Whole Town's Talking* was produced in the early 1950s, its call for community action would seem consistent with the social impetus of the 1960s and the historical moment that produced public television legislation. Lyndon Johnson introduced the Public Television Act on February 28, 1967, seeking Senate support for a national television system dedicated to broadcasting in the public interest. In his fourth message to Congress on health and education, Johnson reported that his administration had recently provided night school programs for 150 high school dropouts in Edmonds, Washington; measles immunizations for 52,000 children in Detroit; and medical care for 6.4 million Americans on welfare. He called for increased funds for medical research, Head Start, computers in classrooms, neighborhood literacy programs, and the National Endowment for the Arts. Wrapped in this appeal for schools, hospitals, and the arts was a recommendation that Congress develop a

> vital and self-sufficient noncommercial television system. . . to instruct, inspire and uplift our people. . . . We have only begun to grasp the great promise of this medium, which, in the words of one critic, has the power to "arouse our dreams, satisfy our hunger for beauty, take us on journeys, enable us to participate in events, present great drama and music, explore the sea and the sky and the winds and the hills." (*Cong. Rec.* 1967: 4642)

Johnson's recommendations were twofold: to establish a Corporation for Public Television and fund its programs initially at $9 million for fiscal year 1968; and to increase Educational Television Facilities Act funding for 1968 to $10.5 million. Beyond this one-year funding request of $19.5 million—minuscule in comparison to the $4.5 billion authorization for military action in Vietnam being debated in the Senate—LBJ offered neither a program for permanent financing nor a structure for the new television system (*Cong. Rec.* 1967: 4642; "Escalation by Whatever Name" 1967: 16). These crippling deficiencies in project planning continue to haunt public broadcasting. Even so, the Public Television Act of 1967 was groundbreaking legislation that pushed noncommercial broadcasting into uncharted terrain. Almost overnight, educational television evolved from an informal group of discrete noncommercial stations funded independently to become, at least conceptually, a network with a national purpose receiving federal funding for programming. It had joined Johnson's Great Society.

A Creative (Paternal) Federalism

Robert Collins notes that LBJ began to invoke the phrase "Great Society" in early 1964 to describe his domestic goals: "a society of success without squalor, beauty without barrenness, works of genius without the wretchedness of poverty" (1994: 23). On May 22, 1964, in a commencement address at the University of Michigan, the president introduced his expansive hopes for a Great Society, which would rest on "abundance and liberty for all." "I do not pretend," he admitted to the graduates, "that we have the full answer to the problems. . . . But the solution to these problems . . . will require a creative federalism" (qtd. in Andrew 1998: 13). The details, he said, would come later.

When the 89th Congress adjourned in October 1966, LBJ had asked for 200 major pieces of legislation; Congress had approved 181 of them. Johnson's proposals sought to remedy a range of social ills, addressing civil rights, poverty, education, health, housing, pollution, the arts, cities, occupational safety, consumer protection, and mass transit (Andrew 1998: 13). The bulk of Johnson's Great Society legislation became law during the years 1964–66. These bills included, among others, the Civil Rights Act (1964), the Voting Rights Act (1965), the Economic Opportunity Bill (1964), the Appalachia Aid Bill (1965), the Medicare Bill (1965), the Elementary and Secondary Education Act (1965), the Higher Education Act (1965), the Housing and Urban Development Act (1965), the Child Protection Act (1966), and the Water Quality Act (1965). All were designed to address perceived human need, although some would later fail due to poor program planning, lack of funding, inability to make significant structural change, or outright dismantling by conservatives. Even so, these legislative acts were united by the mainstream idealism and social altruism of the moment in which they were created, and were characterized by widespread commitments to a national community. As Marshall Kaplan and Peggy Cuciti suggest, this commitment muted divisions of class and race and recognized "responsibility for improving the position of the least advantaged and for shaping the quality of the physical and social environments, its willingness to experiment and to be evaluated and finally its trust in government as the lever for achieving desired change" (qtd. in Andrew 1998: 198).

As an instrument of public enlightenment, noncommercial television cohered philosophically with the programs of the Great Society, especially arts and education initiatives. Not only did educational broadcasters share LBJ's commitment to providing quality education for all the nation's children, there was also increasing attention to ways to make the performing arts a focus of American lives. To this end, LBJ sponsored more than seventy bills promoting the arts and humanities. Legislation was proposed and passed that funded councils, touring companies, and national organizations supporting local and regional arts efforts. The national impulse that created the National Foundation on the Arts and Humanities in 1965 would also form the Corporation for Public Broadcasting in 1967. As the Carnegie Commission wrote:

> Public Television can open a wide door to greater expression and cultural richness for creative individuals and important audiences. . . . Public Television programs should show us domains of learning, emotion, and doing, examples of skill, human expressiveness, and physical phenomena that might otherwise be outside our ken. It should bring us new knowledge and skills, lifting our sights, providing us with relaxation and recreation, and bringing before us glimpses of greatness (1967: 93–94).

Public Television Legislation:
Flaws in Focus and Timing

The Public Television Act was offered up in a moment of great social change. Even so, its potential to develop as a significant force in U.S. culture was severely constrained by the particular social and political environment in which it was introduced. Presented late in Johnson's presidency, after passage of extensive reform measures that had pulled support from both sides of the aisle, public TV would be aligned with more peripheral arts programs. Although plans for a public television bill began in late 1964, public broadcasting was not included in any Great Society reform legislation addressing long-range social issues, such as adult illiteracy, voting rights, school desegregation, and educational reform. As important as elite and middle-class culture were, it was education, civil rights, and the war on poverty that reached into the places where people lived and anchored the futures of their children. In the 1960s—especially as education took on a new reformist tone—these were the arenas most likely to instantiate public television within the infrastructure of American society.

The timing of the Public Television Act was inauspicious. Voted into law on the eve of 1968, it was subsumed by events that would, by the end of the year, mark the decline of a liberal movement begun with the election of John Kennedy in 1960. Johnson's guns-and-butter policy had brought the U.S. treasury to the brink of bankruptcy; the war in Vietnam had become a national nightmare; and Martin Luther King Jr. and Robert Kennedy lay dead at the hands of assassins. Nineteen sixty-eight began with the Tet offensive; it ended with the election of Richard Nixon as president.

> [I]n the course of the year . . . many who had turned one last time to the political process for deliverance abandoned hope in it. Some did persevere afterward in the anti-war and civil rights movements, but the consensus reading of the year, reflected in most journalistic postmortems, was that the events of 1968 had left liberalism in ashes. (Witcover 1998: 21)

Nixon took office in January 1969. His election marked the beginning of a new political conservatism and the close of a period that could have witnessed not only engaged social action by public TV, but also adequate, protected, and long-term federal funding for the project. When introducing the Public Television Act in February 1967, LBJ had promised, "Next year, after careful review, I will make . . . proposals for the Corporation's long-term funding" (*Cong. Rec.* 1967: 4642). Those funding proposals would never come; and within four years, Richard Nixon would mount a sustained attack on public broadcasting that culminated with a presidential veto of the 1972 funding authorization and conservative control of the CPB board (Blakely 1979: 204–5).

Finally, LBJ's own brand of centrist liberalism doomed public television's role as an agent of grassroots change. John Andrew III writes that under Johnson's leadership, the Great Society functioned as a top-down, paternalistic movement that "cast government as the elite-dominated problem-solver"; Johnson "could never understand . . . why various minorities refused to recognize that he had their best interests at heart. Why wouldn't they let him 'do good,' not only *for* them but *to* them?" (1998: 10). Further, LBJ's strategy attacked structural problems by introducing new programs and leaving existing institutions intact; few efforts mirrored the local participation, and possibilities for real change, of the controversial Community Action Program (CAP) and its Community Action Agencies (CAA). David Broder notes that Johnson mistook lack of debate for consensus government, when in fact the Great Society was largely a "hand-me-down government carried to its ultimate expression, with bounties, benefits, and, of course, directions issuing from the top" (qtd. in Andrew 1998: 195). Johnson's preference for a top-down and benevolent federalism over a participatory, discussion-oriented governance model framed his remarks to the Senate on February 28, 1967: "I am convinced that a vital and self-sufficient noncommercial television system will not only instruct, but inspire and uplift our people" (*Cong. Rec.* 1967: 4642). Even in the waning moments of the Great Society, Johnson's image of government as teacher, preacher, and provider held.

Hailed in 1967 as a social institution "whose time had come," public television would ultimately be compromised by its late induction into the Great Society, its inclusion within a top-down concept of governance, and its introduction in a moment of social upheaval, violence, and deepening cynicism. One can only speculate how public television might have developed had its timing and focus been different—had it aligned itself early on with elements of social change (civil rights, the war on poverty, health and education reform) and come before the

American public in 1964–66, rather than 1967. Not only might the system have developed deeper alliances with American constituencies and
grassroots groups, but the always problematic battle for funding might
have been waged before a sympathetic, liberal administration instead of
a conservative and distrustful one.

The Ford Foundation: Patron with an Agenda

You are the leaders in educational television broadcasting. . . . If
you succeed, the advancement of the Great Society we seek will
be strongly assisted. I wish you well.

—Lyndon B. Johnson, letter to C. Scott Fletcher,
December 4, 1964

Johnson's letter to Fletcher arrived as educational broadcasters were
convening in Washington, D.C., for the First National Conference
on the Long-Range Financing of Educational Television Stations on
December 7–9, 1964. The convention, organized by Fletcher as acting head of Educational Television Stations (ETS), initiated a wide-
ranging discussion of noncommercial TV's purpose and funding and
set in motion a national presidential study of educational television
in the United States. Financed by the Carnegie Corporation of New
York and developed by a blue-chip commission of business, arts, education, and government elites, the report would become the basis of
the 1967 Public Television Act.

Although the Ford Foundation was not listed as principal sponsor of
either the 1964 meeting or the presidential study, both bore witness to
the foundation's long-standing philanthropic commitment to ETV. Indeed, without Ford Foundation support, it is likely that neither the
conference nor the study would have been conducted. The conference
was planned by ETS, a recipient of several large Ford Foundation
grants, and the Carnegie Corporation had been recruited by Ford to
fund the presidential study. This behind-the-scenes maneuvering on
behalf of educational television was consistent with the level of assistance provided over time by the foundation's directors, who had perceived the educational and cultural potential of noncommercial television before many educational broadcasters. However, Ford's
contribution came with a price. Just as Johnson's definition of the

Great Society limited the development of U.S. public broadcasting, so too did the social and cultural agenda of the system's most generous donor.

Ford Foundation Funding

The Ford Foundation's financial support of noncommercial television had depth and longevity. By 1963 Ford had invested more than $80.7 million in the projects and programs of educational TV: $7.5 million by the Fund for Adult Education (FAE), $10 million by the Fund for the Advancement of Education, and $63.2 million by the foundation itself. In 1965 the Ford Foundation initiated a new program, Matching Grants to Community Stations, which allocated $20.5 million to thirty-seven stations. The following year, it appropriated $10 million to help develop the Public Broadcast Laboratory and provided another $6 million for national program development (Blakely 1979: 169–70).

The Ford Foundation's earliest grants to ETV were made in 1951, when the FAE, with Fletcher as chair, focused on spectrum space for noncommercial television, funding both the NAEB and JCET in the campaign for noncommercial reservations. Having helped secure 242 dedicated channels for education, the FAE went on to produce matching grants that established all but one of the first thirty educational TV stations, at between $100,000 and $150,000 per station (Fletcher 1973: 15). Importantly, Fletcher also persuaded FCC chair Paul Walker to waive the commission's 1952 stipulation that noncommercial stations had but one year to make application and produce evidence of funding before their allocations reverted to commercial status:

> I [Fletcher] said to chairman Paul Walker, "You're just about killing us all. Won't you give us an extension?" He said, "No. It was in the original contract or arrangement that you would have to show ample proof of dedicated attitudes on the part of the key people in education about educational television and by that . . . I mean cash, equipment, and applications for licenses." (Fletcher 1973: 21)

Fletcher asked the JCET to set up a dinner meeting for all members of the commission: "I said it was imperative for every member to be present except for an exceptional situation or illness. I wanted to get a unanimous vote that night by the FCC. Everyone was present" (Fletcher 1973: 21). Fletcher's recommendation, accepted by both the FCC and educational broadcasters, established the Ford Foundation as power broker, patron, and behind-the-scenes engineer for the fledgling educational system: "My proposal to them was, that if you will waive the one-year time limit, we will guarantee thirty stations on the air within three to four years. We will also guarantee the continuation of a national programming service known as the Educational Television and Radio Center" (Fletcher 1973: 21). For almost two decades, the Ford Foundation made useful, progressive, even life-saving contributions to the developing noncommercial broadcasting system. Early on, the FAE financed experimental programming concepts in radio and television. It also funded conferences, meetings, and media research, including the Midwest Airborne Television Instruction Program, which explored ways videotaped transmissions from airplanes could enhance classroom teaching. Although this project, funded at $13 million by Ford, was finally discontinued, it was one of the first experiments in anticipation of satellite systems (Blakely 1979: 162).

As promised, the FAE developed and financed the Educational Television and Radio Center (ETRC). Designed by Fletcher and a committee comprised of George Stoddard (Columbia University), Harold Lasswell (Yale University), Robert Calkins (Brookings Institution), and Ralph Lowell (trustee of Boston's Lowell Institute), the ETRC was incorporated on November 21, 1952. Its twelve-member, all-male board of directors fulfilled Fletcher's dream of involving "top figures in scholarship, education, social science, communications, arts, business management, and program production" in building a national ETV production house (Blakely 1979: 103). Harry Newburn, president of the University of Oregon and Stoddard's nominee for the new ETRC post, was named president of the center in 1953. Newburn insisted that the ETRC be established at the University of Michigan, and under his leadership, the new national organization took on an overtly educational mission: "Foremost, an educational television program must in fact be educational; it must effect changes in the viewer of an educational nature." Further, said Newburn, the center's programs should "supplement and enrich local program activities, not take the place of them." (qtd. in Blakely 1979: 104). The ETRC began occasional programming service on January 1, 1954. There was slow but steady growth in the numbers of programs it produced, from four and three-quarters hours in 1954 to five hours in 1955, five and three-quarters hours in 1956, and seven and one-half hours in 1957 (Blakely 1979: 105).

Public media historians Robert Blakely (1979: 112) and James Day (1995: 68) both record antagonisms between noncommercial stations and the ETRC. Not only was Newburn viewed as having a "university president" style of management that neglected broadcast quality for academic content, but there was little communication between stations and the center. Blakely reports that the rift between the "ETRC, a rootless national agency, and the stations rooted in the communities" widened, provoking a final confrontation in March 1958 between managers and Newburn at the Affiliates Committee meeting in Biloxi, Mississippi (1979: 130). Newburn tendered his resignation, effective immediately, and returned to academia that fall as president of Montana State University (Day 1995: 69).

Ford Foundation Influence

Newburn's departure precipitated the center's move to New York City. These changes in staff and location ushered in a new era that saw a new national thrust by the center's board and invigorated interest in noncommercial media by the Ford Foundation. The new ETRC president was John F. White, a protégé of Ford Foundation President Henry Heald; his stated goal was to make the center "America's Fourth Network" (Day 1995: 72). Over the next five years, the ETRC would become the National Educational Television and Radio Center (NETRC), receive a series of large Ford Foundation grants to develop further as a national service, and come under even closer scrutiny by foundation staff. As the center evolved to more closely resemble a national network, stations increasingly had less editorial control over the content of programs produced by the NETRC (Blakely 1979: 124). Instead, the foundation itself drove programming direction and decisions.

Initial FAE funding for 1953–56 had included $1 million for operations, $3 million for programming, and the stipulation that at least $2.5 million be used for "programs in international affairs, national or political affairs, economic affairs, and the humanities, including the arts" (Blakely 1979: 103). In addition, all recipients of FAE matching grants were required to be station affiliates of the ETRC. By 1963 foundation directives had become even more specific: the NETRC would not support educational radio, 50 percent of all its television productions would be public affairs programs, and the center would produce (or otherwise acquire) and distribute five hours of high-quality cultural and public affairs programming to all ETV stations each week (Day 1995: 79; Blakely 1979: 128). The foundation's gifts of $10.3 million in 1959–61, $4.7 million in 1962, and $6 million in 1963 provided critical funding for the NETRC in a moment of increasing television production costs. This infusion of capital had its own price, however, as the foundation moved to eliminate educational radio, instructional television, and ancillary station services from the venue of the national production center.

The philanthropic relationship established by Scott Fletcher in 1951 not only put Ford on the line for long-term funding of educational broadcasting, it placed the foundation at the helm of ETV policy and programming initiatives. Through the marshaling of foundation funds, staff, and political influence, the Ford Foundation became increasingly instrumental in the creation of a noncommercial television system in the U.S. Efforts by the FAE led specifically to the allocation of spectrum space, financing of station start-ups, and development of a national production and distribution center. It also put in place institutional procedures that laid the foundation for the organizational infrastructure of the national network, PBS, and the system as a whole. Even more importantly, Ford redefined and expanded noncommercial broadcasting's core identity and public vision, aligning the system's programming strategies and purpose with the philosophies and interests of the foundation and its directors. Central to the Ford Foundation's organizational ideology were commitments to political expertise, the liberal arts, and cultural philanthropy.

The leadership of Fletcher, in particular, would frame noncommercial broadcasting as the nation's cultural custodian. He was adamant that survival of a free society depended upon the informed and responsible action of individuals versed in languages, literature, art, history, and science. Active citizenship, public service, and governance, he said in a 1961 address to the Officers' Club at Tinker Air Force Base in Oklahoma City, demanded a liberal education: "There can be no true democracy without a liberally educated citizenry" (Fletcher Papers, box 4). Fletcher also viewed liberal arts training as essential in the development of executive talent for business, saying it provided managers with the intellectual depth and experience they needed to "measure up." Liberal education, he argued, marked the long-term difference between mediocrity and excellence in executive performance: "The tasks executives have begun to face today and will inescapably confront tomorrow, arising out of the economic and social roles of corporations in American life, are of a magnitude that cannot even be properly grasped, let alone successfully dealt with, except by men with 'big' minds" (Fletcher 1957: viii). If the liberal arts cultivated a "bigness of mind," they also deepened insights "with regard both to men themselves and men in their social relationships" and helped them develop the necessary skills to "more wisely control the world in which they live[d]" (Fletcher 1957: viii). Importantly, liberal arts training was also seen as a source of wisdom, critical sense, and superior values. In chapter 1 of his unpublished manuscript, "The Importance of Liberal Adult Education," Fletcher invoked the ideas of Cordozo to support the goals of the liberal arts tradition:

> What the colleges—teaching humanities . . . —should at least try to give us, is a general sense of what . . . *superiority* has always signified and may still signify. The feeling for a good human job anywhere, the admiration of the really admirable, the disesteem of what is cheap and trashy and impermanent—this is what we call the critical sense, the sense of ideal values. It is the better part of what men know as wisdom. . . . (Fletcher Papers, box 3).

This pursuit of "the really admirable" coheres with Ellen Lagemann's analysis that advocates of liberal studies have typically believed training in the liberal arts grants one the ability to recognize "the best," and to escape "bad taste in living, in music, in drama, in recreation, and, most of all, the utter drabness of unfulfilled lives" (1992: 118). For the Ford Foundation, a liberal arts education granted intellectual depth and critical discernment. Tied inextricably to wisdom, superior judgment, and cultural taste, it was a prerequisite for political leadership, executive management in business, and active citizenship.

The foundation's *Ten Year Report of the Fund for Adult Education* cited two FAE goals: "to help make educational television a reality; and to put it in the service of continuing liberal education" (Ford Foundation 1961: 14). By 1961 these objectives were already becoming a reality. As Chairman of the Board Charles Percy reported:

> Ten years ago there was not one single educational television station in the entire country. Today, to a great extent as a result of the timely leadership and support provided by the Fund, there are over 55 noncommercial educational television stations exploiting and exploring the tremendous potential of the medium for educational and cultural programs (Ford Foundation 1961: 3).

Educational television was not the fund's only venue for promoting a popular liberal arts education for American citizens. Fletcher's office also developed study/discussion groups, community lectures, seminars, and conferences. While Fletcher believed that "liberal education embodies a cluster of values of high significance in themselves" (1957: viii), his agenda as chair of the Ford Foundation's Fund for Adult Education assumed a hierarchy of knowledge and experience that privileged elite culture. His larger project focused on the ways educational TV could train the nation, "purposefully and by design," in the liberal arts tradition.

If the philanthropic altruism of the Ford Foundation narrowed the focus and range of noncommercial television, it also restricted the voices participating in noncommercial broadcasting in the mid-sixties. The National Citizens Committee for Public Television (NCCPTV) was created by the foundation in 1967 to "stimulate all Americans to more vigorous support of public television" ("If Ben Kubasik Calls" 1967: 8). Like other national public television boards of its time, however, the NCCPTV was far from representative of the American population. Headed by Thomas P. F. Hoving, director of the Metropolitan Museum of Art in New York City, the NCCPTV was a roll call of prominence that included 119 "distinguished citizens" from government, publishing, education, commerce, and the arts. Leading lights Paddy Chayefsky, Bill Cosby, John Kenneth Galbraith, Ralph Lowell, Myrna Loy, and Kingman Brewster were among its members (Fletcher Papers, box 6). The membership of the Corporation for Public Broadcasting, announced on February 17, 1968, was similarly impressive.

The board included Dr. Milton Eisenhower, president emeritus of Johns Hopkins University; Dr. James Killian Jr., chairman of the corporation, Massachusetts Institute of Technology; John D. Rockefeller III, chairman of the board of trustees, the Rockefeller Foundation; and Jack Valenti, president of the Motion Picture Association of America ("Corporation for Public Broadcasting" 1967: 311).

Public television's national advisory boards and committees were comprised of elites who shared not only class-specific backgrounds and social influence, but also cultural training and sensibilities. As Hoving noted in his July 12, 1967, address before Congress, NCCPTV members were "not neophytes to the goals and tastes [of] Public Broadcasting programs":

> All of us on the committee have one thing in common. We have had the opportunity to taste of beauty and found it good, and we have courted controversy and, through it, found at least some truth. Most of us on the committee live in the give-and-take world of ideas, whether they be of art or reality, and invariably, these are inextricably intertwined.
>
> We are the lucky ones. We are joining together to see to it that our luck is shared. Many of this nation's citizens catch only glimpses of what we have beheld and, at times, have lived. Others have not even had a chance.
>
> We intend that the National Committee's voices become a choir that will not only sing a viable Public Broadcasting system into existence, but make it as strong and free as it ought to be (Flectcher Papers, box 6).

Hoving's defense of beauty, truth, and the "give-and-take world of ideas" resonated with the values and assumptions of the Carnegie Corporation's People's Institute of the 1930s. These cultural philanthropists, who were working specifically in liberal adult education, sought to expose the wider public to "the best which has been thought and said in the world" in hopes of elevating the standards and tastes of the rank and file. Their aim was to help those of the "undifferentiated mass . . . who [were] capable of becoming something more than automatons" (Lagemann 1992: 118). Hoving's address before the House Commerce Committee carried similar implications of taste engineering, a process dependent upon a graded valuation of knowledge and cultural experiences. In Hoving's analysis, some voices, ideas, and artistic expressions clearly had wider social authority than others; they were better, perhaps even "the best." Many citizens, presumably lacking Hoving's background and training, were not as "lucky" as he and his colleagues on the NCCPTV, had not "tasted of beauty and found it good."

These elitist sentiments, coupled with its reluctance to cultivate local involvement, curtailed the committee's effectiveness as advocate for the new public broadcasting system. Despite its ability to gain the ear of Washington and to produce news coverage in the *New York Times*, the NCCPTV did not achieve widespread and enduring support for a "strong and free" public television. Instead, over a period of two years, the committee lost some of its most powerful members, including industrialist Leland Hazard of Philadelphia, Phyllis Dennery of New Orleans, and Ralph Lowell of Boston ("Citizens TV Group" n.d.; Lowell 1968). Significantly, each had deep and practical ties to the educational station in his or her community, and each viewed the committee as a divisive force within public TV. Each was also disappointed by the exclusion of grassroots groups from NCCPTV. As Dennery wrote to Hoving in her letter of resignation, dated October 28, 1968:

> Among my fondest hopes for the Committee, as you know, was for it to provide the link with thousands of local Trustees around the country who have had little opportunity to meet, exchange ideas on policies and programming and to develop new fundraising techniques, thereby providing greater talent to complement the professional staffs of the Public TV stations. The new thrust of your Committee appears to eliminate any chance of these types of activities under the auspices of the Committee. This I believe to be most unfortunate, as these thousands of Trustees are a great untapped source of support on a national level for Public Broadcasting (Fletcher Papers, box 6).

Local and state PTV boards from around the country attempted to extend their help and involve Hoving in community broadcasting. The Ohio University Public Television-Radio Advisory Committee, for example, suggested that "there are many ideas we could feed on to you," and offered to "act as a local sounding board for ideas germinated at the national level" (Quinn 1967). Unfortunately, like other PTV organizations in the sixties, the NCCPTV would retain its national focus, becoming over time less a champion for public television than a quality watchdog of all American television. As Hoving had noted when he was named chair of the National Citizens Committee, his major concern was the lack of quality programming on American TV: "If we want an enemy, we share a common one: the shoddy, over-popular, banal, mediocre, rinky-dink, hand-me-down, piece-meal, scotch-tape, Mickey Mouse pap of no quality, whether it exists on commercial, noncommercial, educational, public, cultural or not, television. Or wherever else it exists" (Fletcher Papers, box 6).

Focusing on issues of quality and taste instead of community ties, the NCCPTV stood in stark contrast to the National Citizens Committee of Educational Television (NCCET), developed in 1952 as a "strong, separate, independent organization to literally promote the idea of ETV nationally and in communities which are logical station points" (Blakely 1979: 94). Underpinned by commitments to local communities and citizen action, the NCCET established regional field offices and cultivated the support of diverse constituency groups throughout the country. Its membership included the AFL-CIO, National Council of Churches, NAACP, League of Women Voters, PTA, and U.S. Chamber of Commerce, among others. Blakely (1979: 95) credits this grassroots organization with mobilizing the local and regional support that built community ETV stations in New York, Chicago, Los Angeles, San Francisco, and Washington, D.C. Importantly, the NCCET's historical antecedents developed not in the People's Institute, but rather in a radio movement responsive to the desires and visions of such people as the Belle Plaine, Kansas, farmer who wrote to the Kansas State Agricultural College president on March 7, 1922:

Dear Sir:

In case you missed it, will enclose clipping from paper which set me to thinking of a means wherby [sic] I and many other Busy farmers who have an hour or so each day could keep in closer touch with the work you are doing, particularly during Short Course. Perhaps it could be arranged to let us take part in Class Room lectures and possibly discussions, in subjects in which we are interested and in numerous other ways receive benefits which owing to our being unable to leave our work we cannot enjoy. It was my privilege to attend most of one Short Course. Being called home, I did not get to finish and it seems to me if wireless telephone can be put to use along these lines it would enable you to better serve the farmers and be an immense help to us. Perhaps I am rather visionary, But I would appreciate hearing from you in regard to this matter.

Sincerely yours,

Jesse C. Walton

P.S. Have you any estimates on cost of apparattus [sic] for this kind of work? (President's Papers)

Without the interventions of the Ford Foundation, public TV might never have been invented. Ralph Engelman (1996: 136) suggests that only the influence and money of the Ford Foundation persuaded noncommercial broadcasters to venture into television in the early 1950s. None of these early public broadcasters had even applied for TV spectrum allocations during the first FCC reservation rounds in 1948; most saw their mission as rooted in radio technology. This lack of a larger broadcasting vision surfaced in the Rockefeller Foundation's Allerton House seminar, developed in the summer of 1949 to stimulate interest in building a noncommercial television system in the U.S. Project Director John Marshall observed in a memorandum dated July 8, 1949, that the response to new ideas of alternative TV service, especially for unserved audiences, was generally "disappointing. . . . While there were good passages of discussion, the tendency of the group was to fall back on an account of what they were doing [in radio]. . . . There is no sense of vision for TV" (Rockefeller Foundation Papers). With its agenda of nationwide liberal arts instruction and worries about an uninformed citizenry, the Ford Foundation provided not only a workable vision for educational TV, but also $120 million in cash and the hands-on leadership of a highly trained executive staff. Along the way—pursuing what Percy called "a driving dedication to innovation, experimentation, and pioneering" (Ford Foundation 1961: 5)—thirty stations developed into a national television service.

Yet even as the Ford Foundation orchestrated the successful development of educational television, it also used ETV to promote its own cultural values, program interests, and public policy agenda. Recognizing the vast, but yet unrealized, distribution potential of noncommercial TV, the foundation exercised significant editorial control to fill up ETV's broadcast schedule with programs focusing on national and international politics. Under the Ford Foundation's tutelage, public television would become authority television, with a national, not local, story to tell. While this worked to satisfy some of the new system's legitimate interests in public service, it also limited performance on educational television to expert voices. Unlike Father John Harney's WLWL or Kansas State University's KSAC, the ETV envisioned by the Ford Foundation was not a system of community dialogue with roots in the neighborhoods. Rather, nationally prominent producers—Frederick Wiseman, William Buckley, and Fred Friendly—and series such as *Lincoln Center: Stage 5*, *NET Opera Theater Project*, and *New York Playhouse* were granted access to national airwaves. As creative control of noncommercial broadcasting shifted to the Ford Foundation and the elites it represented, the populist movement that had been educational radio's wellspring lost its voice.

Not only did ETV promote the speech, ideas, and public policy interests of the educated and professional classes, it also worked to contain a potentially disruptive popular democracy. Although the Ford Foundation's end goals were citizenship and participatory governance, its philanthropic efforts were undergirded by convictions that the enlightened, liberally educated person was better equipped for community service. As Fletcher noted on page 3 of "The Importance of Liberal Adult Education,"

> [Liberal education] can, by encouraging rational thinking in man, offer invaluable aid in understanding and influencing the direction of economic, political, and social forces. . . . In these rapidly changing times . . . liberal arts training play[s] a critical part in determining *whether or not America will have educated citizens of this sort* (Fletcher Papers, box 3).

While the concept of "quality education for everyone through public television" offered broader and more egalitarian access to liberal education, it was nonetheless framed by the notion that only a rational, educated person was right to govern. For the Ford Foundation, democratic life was not to be left to the vagaries of the political process; it required management through education and cultural instruction. Employing educational TV as a vehicle for general training in liberal arts values, the FAE promoted its own concepts of governance skill and expertise among the American people, teaching them to be "capable" citizens. The focus of the liberal arts on lifelong learning, appreciation of the arts and humanities, and critical thinking positions this educational tradition as useful in democratic practice. The Ford Foundation's sole emphases on liberal education and teaching, however, narrowed the definitions of citizenship and political expertise and limited the voices, perspectives, and programming options of public television. The programming focus of the foundation stressed surveillance of popular democratic expression and worked to instantiate elite experiences and discourses as "the best." Under Ford Foundation cultivation, educational television not only created an expertise-driven public affairs format, but became the purveyor of the high-culture text. While this opened up access to art and literary works to the larger public, it also clearly established these expressions as more worthy discourses, further entrenching a class-based hierarchy of knowledge and taste. This broadcasting practice had widespread social implications because it validated the norms, values, and cultural preferences of upper- and upper-middle-class society, reinforcing class differences in the U.S.

As Pierre Bourdieu (1984: 27) suggests, the consumption of texts is dependent upon cultural capital, competencies learned through formal and "extra-curricular" training and within family systems. Cultural needs, preferences, and practices are the products of upbringing, education, and social class; one's participation with elite texts relies, at least in part, on a measure of socially privileged experience. By introducing a prototypical prime-time, high-quality text into American living rooms—and labeling it as such—public TV produced not only cultural education, but a means of measurement by which viewers could differentiate their own cultural tastes, standards, and social class.

In 1951, educational TV did not exist. There were no stations, no programs, no space on the spectrum. The value of the Ford Foundation's financial contribution in creating this American institution cannot be discounted. Even so, moving through a liberal arts initiative into public policy and taste engineering, the foundation put educational TV to use in meeting its own agenda for U.S. society. Through the influence of the Ford Foundation, noncommercial TV became a proponent of liberal education, an agent of elite artistic and political culture, and a vehicle for the Ford Foundation's definition of American democracy and citizenship—all at the expense of neighborhood needs, minority voices, and popular expression. As essential as the Ford Foundation's monetary and staffing assistance, the price for philanthropic patronage was a shift in institutional character.

Addressing the National Association of Television and Radio Announcers in August 1968, FCC commissioner Nicholas Johnson called for programming that met the needs of American blacks. Seeking to build local community and ethnic identity, Johnson told his audience that top-forty "soul music [was] not enough." Programs should instead showcase black heritage and history, as well as news of the neighborhood. Such a forum for expression, discussion, and dependable information, said Johnson, would improve the everyday lives of the nation's 22 million black citizens:

> Don't tell me your audiences won't listen to useful and interesting information and discussion about what's happening, and how to better their lives. I've got the white man's figures to prove your black listeners are a whole lot more intelligent, upward-striving, and responsive to quality than many black disc jockeys and program directors think. WDAS' Philadelphia survey showed what blacks said they thought was most important to them was not soul music, but housing and slums (37%), jobs and poverty (28%), and education and schools (14%). Think about it. (Johnson 1968: 8)

Johnson's suggestions about how to improve broadcasting service for inner-city blacks included the production of performances by black musicians and documentaries focusing on black history; the use of short jingles to provide information about city services; and the dramatization of original scripts about life in the community (Johnson 1968: 9–12). His ideas were not expensive or impossible. What made them different was a changed emphasis in content: looking at markers of identity and a rich and shared historical past; offering truly vital information about jobs, housing, garbage collection, education, and health care; and creating a space for local self-expression. Seeking neighborly ties in a diverse social arena, Johnson wanted nothing less than an accessible and open-ended public sphere for the black community.

It is significant that the appeal to create such a public space through broadcasting was made, not to public television, but rather to a profit-centered commercial system. The job of improving the daily lives and opportunities of minority populations would seem logically the role of public TV. Not only were its roots buried deep in the community-building legacies of educational radio, but the system's first national series had been predicated on a passion for local and performative talk. As series writer Mayo Simon recalled in *"The Whole Town's Talking*: An Experimental Venture in Educational Television," after viewing the first episode:

> We watched the men and women of this town stand up and talk about their school and their community. We saw their nervousness, their hesitation, their embarrassment. It had probably been a long time since anyone had asked them what they thought—and stayed for an answer. When Larry Gardner got up and cracked his knuckles and said—"A man came around here a couple of years ago and said all the whistle stops will have to go. Well, I don't believe that. I don't believe that's true at all"—when we saw this, we were seeing a magnificent bit of acting by a man who had spent a lifetime preparing to play just one part—himself. (Hull Papers, box 5)

By the time Johnson took the stage in 1968, however, these ties to the common discourses of the neighborhood had been severed. Public television, originating in a populist impulse that privileged the local community, had become an authority figure in U.S. culture, a benevolent distributor of "quality" texts that focused on national arts and politics, and that reinforced class norms and positioned its audience as passive.

If inclusion in the Great Society arts program contained public TV's potential as a change agent, the Ford Foundation's largesse limited its topics and speakers. By the early 1960s the values and institutional purposes of the Ford Foundation had become inculcated in the organizational self-perceptions and established practices of public TV. Under Ford Foundation influence, public television became an expert and distanced authority, and although all Americans were encouraged to listen and learn, few had performance rights. The modern-day polis of *The Whole Town's Talking*, offered on "television film" fifteen years before, had been effectively silenced. Predicated on commitments to popular speech, mutuality, and respect for difference, public TV's earliest series—an experiment in technology and community—disappeared into the Iowa landscape. Lacking a sustained investment in vigorous and local talk, public television relinquished its opportunity to explore how face-to-face democracy could be enacted in and through a roomful of cables, cameras, and participants.

Wagner-Hatfield died on the Senate floor in mid-May 1934, taking with it the broadcast reform movement that had battled network radio and the American political system for space on the spectrum. When the mike opened in the 1960s for a discussion of public media in America, the concepts on offer strongly resembled those that had given rise to the broadcast reform movement of the thirties. As demonstrated by such documents as the Carnegie Commission's *Public Television: A Program for Action*, the conversation coalesced around issues of alternative programming, vigorous debate of public issues, and protected airtime for minority voices. This report championed cultural diversity as a staple of American life, public television as its instrument of expression, and community as the heart of the nation. Following the tradition of *The Whole Town's Talking*, the Carnegie Commission proposed that public TV stimulate popular talk and decision making through the technology of broadcasting. Privileging local performance and grassroots democracy, these early conceptions of public broadcasting sought to construct a problem-solving and participatory community through engaged civic discourse.

As the influences of the late sixties, Johnson's Great Society, and the Ford Foundation culminated to shape the institutional character of noncommercial broadcasting, public TV lost sight of its foundational commitments to local debate and popular expertise. The "People's Instrument" evolved to become not an advocate for participatory democracy and community ties, but a paternalistic, top-down provider of "quality" and expert voices. These tendencies have continued in the years since, as seen in the PBS Democracy Project, developed in 1994 to enhance civic participation. Addressing Americans' general lack of interest in election campaigns and low voter turnouts, public broadcasting joined with other advocates of civic journalism in efforts to improve democratic involvement and reportage ("Renovating Democracy's Feedback Loops" 1996: 1). U.S. citizens, said PBS staff, require more information and increased access to politicians and the political media. The objective of the ongoing PBS project has been to involve voters more directly in the political process, largely through town meetings, documentaries, citizen-oriented reporting, and collaborative efforts by newspapers and public

stations. Even as the Democracy Project has called for viewer participation, crucial decisions about the agenda have been determined
by public television professionals. The choices of topics, speakers,
and salient issues have been made not by the public, but by project
staff. Further, the language of project memos often betrays a well-
intentioned, but lofty and distanced attitude by project editors and
reporters, who are urged to choose stories carefully, based on their
faithful reading of the citizens' agenda. Whenever possible, public
broadcasting staff advise, stories should include citizen voices and de-
scriptions of citizen attitudes. In 1996, one project editor encouraged
his reporters to make at least one call a week to a randomly chosen
citizen to ascertain his or her concerns. Finally, reporters are cau-
tioned not to write and report for other journalists. The Democracy
Project rules urge them to, "Always remember—the listener is a citizen" ("Citizen-Oriented Reporting" 1996: 6).

The goals of the Democracy Project would seem to cohere with
other discourses of civic journalism that call for citizens who are
"reengaged in public life" and "participants in a self-governing society" (Martin 1999: 158; Schaffer 1997: 3). Even so, old roles of teachers and passive, listening students emerge again. As valuable as the
impulse to enable citizenship is, public television's response of
agenda-setting and top-down, documentary reporting fails to stimulate an engaged and useful conversation with American publics. Developed within the system's long-standing self-identity of teacher, authority, and expert speaker, the Democracy Project has seen its goals
of participation eclipsed by public TV's failure to collaborate with
American people as interactive citizen producers. Michael Schudson's
1998 critique that "nothing in public journalism removes power from
the journalists or the corporations they work for" clearly extends to
public television as well (qtd. in Martin 1999: 160).

Even though the Democracy Project won an Angel Award for excellence in media in March of 1997, it had "underwhelming viewer re-
sponses" ("PBS Democracy Project" 1997: 1; "Hume Will Be 'Choreographer'" 1996: 18). Project Director Ellen Hume has acknowledged
this lukewarm response, but she places the onus for the series' low ratings on the viewer, not the program, suggesting that this type of public affairs series demands a certain kind of "quality" viewer: a "citizen"
seeking an "oasis," someone who can "come to a broadcast without the
idea of being entertained" (Bedford 1998:1). American constituencies

could conceivably respond more positively to the Democracy Project if public television were to follow the lead of WBUR, a Boston University radio station that shared control of the spectrum with its listeners in the early 1970s. *Project Drum* was innovative public media practice that allocated a portion of airtime each week to inner city residents. With local people acting as producers and speakers, WBUR created a "radio station within a radio station" and granted the neighborhood performance rights to the air. The project was critically acclaimed: "[WBUR has] met the needs of the ghetto's audience in a dynamic and compelling way. Much that has been learned in Boston could be applied in other places" (Henderson 1970: 29).

That this practice has not been repeated speaks to public broadcasting's general lack of commitment to popular speech. Public television has missed its opportunities to grant American publics working access to the spectrum or any real control in station policy, programming, and production; nor has it put broadcast technology to use in enabling a diverse and talkative public sphere. Instead, the system, abandoning old concepts of public service, has effectively closed the messy, risky, and cable-cluttered public space in which an Iowa farmer reinvented himself through discourse in 1952.

CHAPTER FIVE

The Re-Forming of Public Broadcasting: A Reconstitution of Public Practices

This book is an indictment of public broadcasting's failure to construct itself as an agent of public talk and social reform. The choices that delivered the spectrum to commercial broadcasters by default in 1934, that produced the "TV as teacher" in 1950, and that designed public TV's "quality" text in 1967 have also darkened a progressive vision that could grant public television both the will and the skills to wage important battles for change. The compromises made in 1934, 1950–51, and 1967—as public broadcasters sought a persuasive mainstream argument—have whittled away the system's public mission. Today noncommercial TV lacks the creative energy to move meaningfully in the broad spectrum of American social life. Despite an underpinning philosophy of publicness and the documented practice of visionaries, public television has become a flawed and timid institution that ignores the tenets of a progressive vision. At the same time, it reinvents the course that has compromised its mission over the years.

The preceding chapters have examined three key moments in which public broadcasting commanded a national audience and engaged in a vigorous struggle for resources. This final chapter summarizes the results of that investigation, critiquing public TV practice while providing compelling evidence of a long-standing public media ideology of public service. Finally, public media reform depends on the system's willingness to reinvent itself as a national institution of public life, making commitments to broad-based control of the spectrum, social reform, and popular community.

Historic Underpinnings of Publicness

Public broadcasting has long been seen as having potential to invigorate important discussions and to promote a just and participatory society. Scholars and practitioners alike have looked to public broadcasting for leadership in building an adequate public sphere that embraces difference, fosters open debate, and enables purposeful action. Regrettably, these expectations have diminished over time. Today, lacking consistent goals, commitments, definitions of service, and even a common conversation, public TV flounders. Early in the twenty-first century, many PTV licensees seem united only by a core programming schedule, the need to raise funds at least four times a year, and a common history.

Suggesting that wider knowledge of that common history could contribute usefully to public media's internal cohesiveness and public service, this book is an effort to reclaim a part of public television's past, to excavate traces of an institutional mission rooted in public purpose, and to demonstrate how specific policy choices compromised public television's institutional vision. Public television's failure to claim a compelling vision prevents the system from meeting its potential and hinders development of useful, problem-solving discourse in U.S. culture. Some observers have pointed to the historical absence of a charter, constitution, or point-by-point plan as evidence of public TV's failed vision, suggesting that U.S. public broadcasting has always functioned without a public mission. On the contrary, although early public broadcasters worked without a formal mission statement, they shared some general beliefs that radio and television should enable public speech, community attachments, and democratic practice. The papers of many early public broadcasters reveal arguments and strategies that position public broadcasting as an institution with a sustaining public purpose and a world view valuing citizen action, critical discussion, and multiple voices. My goal has been to reclaim the central tenets of that philosophic road map.

Although decades apart and situated in different social and political environments, each of the three key moments explored in the preceding chapters involved an important fight for resources; each encapsulated noncommercial broadcasting's central arguments; and each engendered action that moved public media into a world of policy and capital. These three events also figured in a common conversation about public life and public media, as the dominant discourse of public media advocates coalesced around ideas of a participatory public, cultural diversity, vigorous public discourse, and citizen access to speech and governance. Commitments to an active public life surface time and again as the philosophic base of the Wagner-Hatfield Amendment in 1934, the FCC hearings of the fifties, and the Public Broadcasting Act of 1967. Although many broadcasting histories have largely ignored these social, intellectual, and philosophic commitments, the discourse of public broadcasting pioneers offers evidence of a collectively understood and accepted sense of vision. As Ralph Engelman (1996: 13) and Joseph Welling suggest, it was a vision originating in early public notions of American broadcasting that viewed the airwaves as a tool for participatory democracy and bound broadcasters in a "direct creative relationship to the communities they serve[d]" (Welling 1996: 21).

Public broadcasting archives offer the memos, reports, letters, speeches, diaries, news accounts, and videos of several hundred men and women who have produced compelling public interest broadcasting over the last seventy years. Like Hartford Gunn (WGBH/Boston), Donley Feddersen (WTIU/Indiana University), and a small group of station managers who worked together to refine the system's "Declaration of Principles" in December 1978, these public broadcasters valued cultural diversity, commonality, and democratic discourses:

> The strength of our nation depends on the ability of our people to govern themselves wisely. Only an informed and enlightened citizenry can shape its own future and assert the inalienable rights of individuals while guarding the essential interests of society. Knowledge and understanding are the foundations of a democracy.
>
> Public television offers a unique means for ensuring the integrity of these foundations. Owned and governed by nonprofit public institutions and motivated by the desire to respond to the needs of the public,

it attempts to reflect the diversity of our people, the richness of our heritage, and the vitality of our culture; to provide a forum for many points of view; and to illuminate the common bonds that tie all mankind together.

We believe it is to the benefit of the American people . . . to ensure that such service shall exist to give voice to the needs, the interests, and the aspirations of all the people, and that they shall be free and independent from interference or control by those who would use them for their own purposes. ("A Declaration of Principles" 1980: 10)

They valued community governance of the airwaves, like Robert Blakely, who adopted "broadcasting for public purposes" as the most descriptive term for public broadcasting:

Broadcasting for public purposes is new, incomplete, malnourished and neglected. But it holds the seeds of larger things. Its potentialities will be discovered and developed only as large numbers and many groups of the American people come to regard it, not as an *institution*, but as *their instrument* to use for the purposes that matter most to them. (Blakely 1971: 10; italics in original)

And they valued popular expression, like Ira Robinson: "To my mind the radio is the voice of the public" (1930:9).

These commitments to community and to socially responsible public speech resonate powerfully with theories of the public sphere. An implicit argument for publicness, these texts and the ideas and beliefs uniting them position public broadcasting as an institution with responsibilities to public life. Lying clearly outside the mainstream of capitalist media, public broadcasting is viewed by many working inside the system as an institution with a public mission.

Moments of Failed Resolve

Despite the dominant discourse of public media's proponents, however, the conversation about noncommercial broadcasting has never been fixed, homogeneous, or uncomplicated. Indeed, as this book has shown, Wagner-Hatfield, the FCC spectrum allocations, and the Public Broadcasting Act served as centers of debate over the direction and policies of U.S. broadcasting in general. In each case, a failure of resolve prevented public media's full development as an agent of the public sphere. Just as the history of U.S. public media is a narrative of visionary voices, it is also an American tragedy, a tale of loss, waste, and failed potential. During three historical moments, the philosophy and structure of nonprofit media took center stage, and the national conversation turned to issues of spectrum control, educational reform, and popular community. Despite the promise of the moment, broadcast reformers made choices that supported the status quo; their chances for increased resources and greater social influence slipped away. The Great Depression, the Red Scare, and the 1960s each provided a social landscape in which to debate and direct the future of democratic media. Tragically, in each instance, public media abdicated responsibility as change agent and narrowed the public sphere.

Re-Forming Public Television

The losses of 1934, 1950–51, and 1967 jeopardized public broadcasting's sense of self, and the organization that survives today is barely recognizable as the talkative, diverse, and public service–oriented medium begun in the 1920s. Yet public television is far from unredeemable. Research for this book began during the congressional funding battles of 1995–96 as a search for public media purpose. As a communications professional who had begun a public television career in the mid-1970s, I believed that a vision for the system existed, that proof of its vigor could be discovered in public media discourses, and that the evidence I uncovered could be used to argue for continued public funding for public broadcasting. In the course of my research, I also discovered compromises that negatively affected public television's organizational character and the culture of its workplace.

These findings are presented here as a way to expand our understanding of U.S. public broadcasting history. Although the scholarly literature focusing on historical and critical approaches to public media is growing, too little now exists. My objective has been to add meaningfully to this body of work. I have also been interested in contributing to discussions about public TV practice and the possibilities for reform. My research and my personal knowledge of many people affiliated with public broadcasting have convinced me that despite public media's failings, reform is possible. By pulling from discursive resources of the past and forming a commitment to viable civic action in the present, public broadcasting can yet become an organization of public purpose.

The public media concept advanced here is informed by the philosophic commitments of Arendt, Habermas, Dewey, and other scholars of the public sphere, all of whom speak of the great value of vigorous discourse, community ties, and the protected spaces of a working polis. In my analysis, democratic media are critically defined by an allegiance to engaged public talk, the use of broadcasting to advance social reform, and efforts to cultivate a broad-based, popular community. Public broadcasters must have deep commitments to public and performative speech, citizen participation, and inclusive and talkative communities. They must desire the "stretchable nets of kinship" (Anderson 1983: 6) that embrace the wide range of human differences and shared experiences. They must acknowledge and pursue the use of broadcasting to advance the public good, and importantly, they must recognize that the recovery of public mission for U.S. public media requires its reconstitution through altered practice.

Some have suggested that public broadcasting's problem is an image problem, that new talk about an old vision will restore its viability. I disagree. Discourse alone cannot recreate public TV's public mission. It must be constructed through thoughtful and purposeful action, as individuals work together to rebuild a broadcasting system founded on publicness and community.

What follows, then, is a program for public media work designed to perform public service and restore public practices. Addressing ways public television can develop as a national institution of publicness, these six concepts work to enable the public speech of American constituencies, to build inclusive communities, and to employ broadcasting as a change agent. Throughout this analysis, public service broadcasting is perceived as a vehicle by which private individuals become public citizens who seek to advance the common good through action; and although local voices are seen as critical for democracy and citizenship, public television's special contribution is the weaving of these voices into a national conversation. This plan for reform is not presented as a plank-by-plank platform for restructuring U.S. public media; it is offered instead as a dialogic and process-oriented contribution to talk about how public television can become a vital and functioning agent of public life in the twenty-first century.

1. Public television must find new ways to grant individuals and constituencies space on the spectrum, access to public speech through public media.

Hannah Arendt (1958: 18) stresses the importance the ancient Greeks attached to civic discourse, conducted within a protected public space that promotes participation, difference, and shared commitments to the body at large. The work of the polis, underpinned by commitments to public talk, is also the work of public television. The needs of American people to speak and be heard in matters of national and local import must become a priority for public broadcasters. It is not enough to subtitle *Sesame Street* and the evening news. Public television must wire the neighborhoods. This could involve commitments to microradio, PEG channels, and closed-circuit cable. It could manifest itself in the dedication of specific blocks of public television airtime or of a second channel to constituency groups. Such practice, however, would fly in the face of public television's sustaining self-identity as teacher and expert. To wire the barrio is to grant its citizens the right to produce and distribute their own messages; to enable this action, public television must not only relinquish its position as sole proprietor of the public airwaves, it must reinvent itself as an agent of diversity.

That this model resembles cable access practice seems clear. However, to offer this challenge to public television in 2003 is not to appropriate the public access mission, but to reclaim an old project of public TV. Experimentation with portable video and a commitment to diverse local voices—both defining characteristics of access TV— were taking hold in the early 1970s at several PBS stations. Programs such as San Francisco's *Open Studio* and *Take 12* in Philadelphia invited local groups to broadcast their views free of charge, and Boston's *Catch 44*, begun in 1971, is seen as a particularly "important precedent in public access television" (Engelman 1990: 4). Public television's commitments to access TV would peak and fade quickly, however, forcing U.S. community television to look elsewhere (primarily Canada) for early leadership (Engelman 1990: 4–10). In the years since, public speech and cultural diversity have been sustaining commitments of public access television and community radio. Both have sought to invigorate democratic media practice in the U.S.

Despite the similarities between the public access model and my own ideal for public TV, important differences of resources, distribution structure, viewer access, and mission exist. Engelman (1996: 264–65) notes that public access was a "historical accident" of the 1970s, growing out of the intersection of technological development in portable video and the expansion of cable TV. Seeking to legitimate and differentiate itself in U.S. culture, and following FCC directives to provide free channels for public use, cable took on the promotion and support of public access. In 2003 this support has dwindled, resulting in precarious funding and threats of cancellation. Since almost all funding for access is provided by cable systems and is capped at 5 percent of gross revenues, funds for these stations and their projects have been minimal (Briller 1996: 56).

Moreover, public access channels are subject to change or even removal from the air. In 1996, for example, Briller (57) reported that TCI Cable in Westchester County, New York, had canceled its county-wide access channel on grounds that the cable system did not have adequate assignments to carry local broadcast stations, pay-for-view, a shopping channel, and public access. Because it neither fit FCC "must carry" rules nor provided income, cable access was the one to go. With the recent acquisition of TCI by AT&T, even more access stations—from Albuquerque to Pacifica, California—face radical reductions in funding. Finally, although community TV operates in a number of American cities and towns—serving a cultural mix in Manhattan; the Lakota, Dakota, Mandan, and Annishinable Indian nations; the City of Chicago; and rural Montana—public access is largely unused. According to the Twentieth Century Fund Task Force on Public Television, between 80 and 90 percent of all PEG assignments are as yet unclaimed (Twentieth Century Fund 1993: 20). U.S. public access is severely underfunded, underutilized, and at risk of being denied channel assignments. Although underfunded and underutilized itself, public television is better equipped to serve some broadcast needs in a community, simply because it has a larger resource base.

Second, public broadcasting is a network that offers a national sub-structure for acquiring, distributing, and promoting programs. With 347 stations in all fifty states, public TV is capable of achieving almost 100 percent penetration of U.S. television markets; a text broadcast nationally has the potential to be viewed by millions of people. Public television's multistation organization—with its satellite interconnections, state networks, ITFS links, and ethnic consortiums—offers a broad-based structure for joining many voices in local, regional, and national conversations. Cable access stations, on the other hand, are expressly local, tied to specific markets.

Third, although public signals are at times distributed by cable systems, public television is rightly seen as a broadcast service, not a cable service. Public television broadcasts its programs free over the public airwaves. It is not a subscription service, and its programs are therefore more broadly available than those of public access, which air solely on cable systems. Although cable television is an industry with outlets throughout the United States, there are still millions of people who do not subscribe to cable TV. Black and Bryant (1996: 374) estimate that almost 40 percent of the U.S. population does not receive cable; this includes many rural residents, single parents, elderly people, and lower income families. Community television producers face the dilemma that confronted early access organizers thirty years ago; their programs had been developed to serve the needs of the poor, who were unable to receive them due to the cost of subscribing to cable TV. Public television, broadcasting an over-the-air signal, is a universal medium serving more of the social spectrum.

Finally, public television has an explicitly public mission, for which it has received public funds and has public obligations, including widespread public access to expression through broadcasting and the furthering of a public agenda. The public sphere theorized by Arendt, Habermas, and Dewey has commitments to individuals who speak and act on behalf of the common good. A polis is seen as a protected zone where private individuals develop solutions to public problems. Even the empowering of individual voices, as proposed here, is seen as public work, since it advances the larger collective good. I envision, for example, children who gain a sense of self-worth by producing videos set to their own music and Hispanics who articulate the politics of the border through the *corrido*. These independent creative projects, originating from a sense of publicness, differ from the performances often seen on public access, which privilege the goals of First Amendment speech and the politics of individual expression.

Service to a range of publics, cultural diversity, freedom of speech, and programs for people at the margin are concepts of a public vision. It is only appropriate that Americans should have more than one outlet for democratic speech in their communities, and the overlap of public broadcasting channels and cable access stations here would seem useful. At the same time, public broadcasting has the resource base, technological structure, and underpinning public vision necessary to support the engagement of many voices debating the public good. As Dewey (1927: 126) suggested seventy-five years ago, this kind of cohesive public program, employing public resources and public talk, is necessary if the Public is to call itself into being through a recognition of common problems and shared, indirect consequences.

2. Public television must encourage popular performance and televisual literacy.

Public television should act on its ability to develop self-reflexivity, critical inquiry, and eloquent discourse. Collaborating with community networks and local storytellers, public TV must find ways for local people to perform as citizen producers. Issues of media, culture, democracy, and the economy—as well as textual strategies of script, framing, representation, lighting, and program scheduling—should become common discourse among Americans. Public television professionals should encourage this critique within both the public media community and the broader culture. Children, especially, should come to understand the role television plays in shaping their perceptions, perpetuating stereotypes, and narrowing diversity. They should also be encouraged to do public-spirited work and to appreciate the potential of public media for social change. Finally, like all Americans, young people should learn to use public media as a means of self-expression and growth, a vehicle for learning to command an audience and to invent new ideas through discourse.

Long an advocate of "outreach," public TV can play a vital role in this enterprise, working to increase individuals' media literacy, video and multimedia production skills, and everyday access to media technology. By putting portable video cameras on the streets, making public TV studios and staff available to local people, and helping people learn to express themselves adequately—even eloquently—on television, public television can enable the voices of the community.

Enhanced private speech will surely be a benefit of this performative venture. The artistic expressions of individual media producers will improve; individuals will be encouraged to invent and reinvent their own subjectivities as they speak themselves into new roles and realities (Richards 1993: 42). More importantly, however, private people will gain skills in articulating and negotiating the needs of the collective through the dominant media. Striving to help people develop social eloquence, the ability to speak well in public, public broadcasting can also help improve the quality of public discourse in general and political discourse in particular. As individuals become more articulate—developing more egalitarian, persuasive, and powerful rhetorical skills—they may also become more civil. This has potential not only for enhancing social life, but for improving the quality of political processes. As W. Barnett Pearce suggests, "At least part of this intangible barrier [between citizens and political life] is a pattern of discourse so fractured that citizens are frustrated in their attempts to take a turn in the public conversation. The quality of public discourse . . . drives the people out of politics" (Pearce and Littlejohn 1997: 90).

Finally, and perhaps most important, social eloquence can enlarge the environment for difference. According to Richard Sennett (1974: 268), a casualty of a disintegrating public sphere is tolerance for difference. With a diminished public culture, relationships and discourses of difference cannot be maintained (Sennett 1974: 61). Humans discover they lack the mechanisms to communicate with individuals who vary in culture, ethnicity, or ideology. Social eloquence—the learned skills of quality public discourse—can help carve out a space for tolerance, a zone in which "people are able to learn a new self-respect, a deeper and more assertive group identity, public skills, and values of cooperation and civic virtue" (Evans and Boyte 1992: 17).

3. Public television must make a commitment to invigorated, broad-based national–local discourse.

As an agent of authentic public life, public television should attack the trends that have allowed a shrinking public sphere to become the norm throughout American culture, in small towns and our nation's cities alike. Educational broadcasters addressed this in 1952, when they enabled, through television technology, a vigorous discussion of common problems and then broadcast *The Whole Town's Talking* throughout the country. The Runnells, Iowa, water supply was a local problem, solved through local discourse; but the processes of the solution—spontaneous, vigorous, and performative speech—were national. As people in rural Iowa gathered to talk, it was participatory democracy in action. To watch from elsewhere, even on kinescope, was, and is, to affirm allegiances to a civil civic life.

As humans, we are members of many communities. They are defined by interests, history, geography, and the elastic spaces of our minds and imaginations. They are local and national; some are both, and one of public TV's great contributions would be to help us know our world, understand our neighbors, and experience the life of these communities through television. Local and national communities are not bipolar entities. They are connected to one another on a shifting continuum; their borders blur. Public television, unlike public access, has a structure of stations, satellite interconnections, and national program centers in place that could allow us to share meanings, debate common problems, and talk about differences across space, in time.

James Curran has suggested that effective public service broadcasting may be tied in this century to a new model that organizes outlets for private enterprise, social markets, and professional and civic sectors around a core of general-interest TV channels. The structure, he says, will satisfy "minority concerns" and "majority pleasures" (1996: 105). This concept also seems helpful in discussing how public broadcasting can situate itself in the social landscape and contribute usefully to public life. Communities, whether local or national, are sites of struggle and difference. They represent a range of voices and experiences, often in tension with one another. Curran's model would not only allow the voices of these many constituencies to be heard, but would facilitate public debate over causes of and social solutions for injustice. This public service paradigm produces and distributes programs for specific audiences, and employs interactive media to develop a broad-based, national conversation.

Writing in the late 1950s, Raymond Williams suggested that a "good community, a living culture, will . . . make room for [and] actively encourage all and any who can contribute to the advance in consciousness which is the common need" (1958: 334). As public television enters the twenty-first century, it stands uniquely poised to enable solidarity, justice, and the "good community" in American culture: to produce a common stock of shared experiences and put in place mechanisms that encourage social critique and engage difference.

4. Not only must public television lose its timidity and learn to take programming risks, it should accept an overtly reformist vision.

Public television is more than a workplace culture; it can and should make a difference in individual lives and U.S. culture. This was clearly the vision of many public broadcasting pioneers, but as the number of public TV visionaries has declined, recollections of their aims and purposes have grown dim. Efforts to rebuild this old passion could legitimately begin with programs for children at risk. Public TV should not only adopt a national agenda of change for American children, but should also allocate real and substantial resources toward development of programs, research, and outreach projects in media literacy and performance. By networking with innovators and other activist groups, writing legislation, developing funding, and granting youngsters a public voice, public television could help kids at the margin survive and prosper.

That public television was not included in most important social reform legislation of the 1960s—especially civil rights—speaks to its neglect of that work in the 1950s. Noncommercial broadcasters skirted opportunities to address "separate but equal" education practices in the early fifties, opting for a mainstream service instead. Choices distancing public broadcasting from important social reform activity of the 1950s would haunt public television a decade later, when the system that developed was seen as peripheral in many Americans' lives. As opportunities emerge in the coming years for substantive social change, public television may again find itself outside the loop because it failed to network with other change agents in the present. Only a dedication to social action now can deter a future on the margins of American political life.

5. Public television must develop a proactive vision of its own that is more than an alternative to commercial broadcasting purpose and practice.

Certainly, there have been useful and legitimate contributions by noncommercial broadcasting in addressing deficiencies of a market-driven commercial system. At the same time, however, educational broadcasting's assumption of a distinctively alternative mission allows commercial broadcasting, not public media, to define the parameters of its identity and service. Cautiously defining its purpose in terms of another's institutional practice, public broadcasting has failed to evolve into a truly unique media service. As Williard Rowland writes, the label "noncommercial" has "implied a negative definition in terms of something else—the dominant, other, commercial system. As such, it [has] carried no sense of positive vision" (1993: 254). Lacking a proactive mission of its own, noncommercial TV has developed as the virtuous—and often boring—cousin of commercial broadcasting, defined as alternative, supplementary, and secondary.

The construction of a coherent, proactive vision within public television could usefully begin with the resurrection of a national organization to facilitate a conversation about mission, vision and visionaries, and programs for action. With the dismantling of NAEB in the early eighties and the subsequent loss of its conferences, seminars, and publications, public television lost a way to talk meaningfully and collectively about the system's history, failings, and prospects. Without a mechanism for institutional self-examination and a broad forum for debate of public purposes, public television lacks a way to address differences among its membership or to invent innovative approaches for public media service. Lacking a blueprint uniquely its own, public television assumes, ironically, the shape and substance of its old nemesis. As television producer Bill Kurtis reports:

> Several executives told me that they didn't regard PBS as a charitable contribution anymore, and they thought cable was filling PBS' programming niche. I could have had any number of corporations underwriting my series (*New Explorers*) if I could have offered them two 30-second spots—then it becomes an advertising buy, like cable, not a charitable donation. How is it "corrupting" PBS when stations al-

ready run 15-second "enhanced underwriting" spots? (qtd. in Hall 1997: 2)

Just as public broadcasting needs its own clearly delineated, progressive, and evolving sense of organizational purpose, it requires new definitions of professionalism. Public broadcasters have long been haunted by the worry that their programs did not measure up to the production standards of the commercial industry. The critique (voiced by commercial broadcasters) that "educators" could not create viable programs surfaced in the 1934 and 1950–51 FCC set-aside hearings; and in the years since, public broadcasting professionals have come to evaluate "professionalism" through the lens of the private sector. In practical terms, this refers not only to creative content, but to eyeballs summoned, dollars raised, and language employed. Increasingly, the terminology of the marketplace dominates the public broadcasting arena, in which public TV professionals have become "entrepreneurs" with "branding" strategies to enlarge their "market share." Noncommercial broadcasting's purposes are service-based, and the system desperately needs values and language that validate that function, and indeed define it as the standard of professionalism and worker identity throughout the system.

6. Public broadcasters must take the lead in demanding structural change in U.S. media.

Stanley Crawford writes of the *acequias*, or irrigation ditches, that channel the waters of the Rio Grande River through the communities of northern New Mexico. These ditches, some dating from the 1700s, are considered property of the community, and access is regulated and enforced. For the farmers who irrigate from the ditch, water is seen as a community good, and those who use it share benefits and obligations that bind them together as a self-conscious public acting on its own behalf. No one has monopoly rights to ditch water. "A narrow channel of water that flows through everybody's back yard" (Crawford 1986: 207), the *acequia* is a public resource.

Similar concepts of publicness—public good, public interest, and public property—guided the development of spectrum law and policy. Douglas Kellner notes that the 1934 Communications Act reinforced the long-standing precedent that broadcasting should be considered "a public good, like air, water, or other elements that belong to everyone, or like parks and highways that can be used by all people" (1990: 185). The premise that radio channels were public property supported a regulatory system that required broadcasters to act in the public interest, convenience, and necessity, and called upon the FRC (and later the FCC) to convene as public stewards to ensure proper use of the spectrum. The concern that monopolists should not possess the airwaves, just as they did not own the country's waterways, resonated in a letter Herbert Hoover wrote to Congress in 1924:

> The decision that the public, through the Government, must retain the ownership of the channels through the air with just as zealous a care for open competition as we retain public ownership of our navigation channels has given freedom and development in service that would have otherwise been lost in private monopolies. (qtd. in *Cong. Rec.* 1927: 2573)

In these early structuring documents of U.S. media policy, the concepts of commonality, conservation, and community benefits clearly applied to radio waves, just as they governed national forests, rivers, wildlife, and rural electricity.

That the large majority of media outlets in the U.S. and abroad are controlled by a handful of conglomerates—so few that their representatives could stand together in one small room—is nothing short of outrageous. As McChesney (2001: 1) notes, this process of global oligopoly is a threat to democratic practice and to an open marketplace of ideas. Clearly, the structure that places broadcast frequencies in the hands of a few global media giants is antithetical to foundational concepts defining the radio spectrum as a natural resource that has public properties, contributes to community life, and requires strict use management.

Public broadcasting's rightful place is at the head of a movement to counter this full-scale privatization of the spectrum and other news and entertainment media. Taking their lead from earlier visionaries—Harry Skornia, Robert Blakely, Hartford Gunn, Dallas Smythe, Clifford Durr, and many others—contemporary public broadcasting professionals are clearly positioned to challenge the status quo. Specifically, public broadcasters can provide genuine service by reinvigorating discussions of publicness in general, and of public service obligations in broadcasting in particular. They can investigate regulatory decisions that delimit media ownership and act as policy watchdogs in making this information known. They can press not only for development of smaller commercial and non-commercial media operations, but also for stricter regulation of commercial media in meeting their public service obligations. Importantly, they can lobby, not for self-sufficiency in the private zone, but rather for full and unencumbered public funding that supports a noncommercial, public service broadcasting sector throughout the country. Recent reports suggest that such efforts would find broad support from the American public. A 1999 study conducted by the Benton Foundation found that although 71 percent of the public reported being unaware that broadcasters receive free access to the airwaves, when told, 54 percent said they favor charging broadcasters for additional spectrum. Further, 79 percent favor a proposal that would require commercial broadcasters to put 5 percent of their revenue into a fund to support public broadcasting (Halonen 1999: 108).

Inclusive and diverse "public interest" discussion groups and task forces established at local, regional, and national levels—as well as a broad national study resembling early Carnegie Foundation recommendations for public broadcasting—could get the ball rolling. Time, as so many have acknowledged, is running out.

At the June 17, 2000, morning session of a national conference on "Public Broadcasting and the Public Interest," a professional from Maine Public Broadcasting rose and angrily defended the public television system, charging that the conference critique of public broadcasting treated innovators unfairly. There was good work going on—in Maine, if nowhere else, she said.

It has not been my intent to suggest that there is a total absence of strong public service broadcasting in the United States. That is clearly not the case. Albuquerque's *Colores* has explored Hispanic culture, especially as it relates to the Southwest, for more than twenty years. In April 2002 KCTS/Seattle launched *Don't Buy It*, a kids-oriented series with a media literacy focus to help children ages nine to eleven recognize the ploys of advertising. The *MacNeil/Lehrer NewsHour* (now *The NewsHour with Jim Lehrer*) premiered in 1975 with the first long-form treatment of television news in the U.S. Despite valid critiques by FAIR [Fairness and Accuracy in Reporting] ("All the Usual Suspects" 1990:1) and Cohen and Solomon (1995: 1) that the show privileges a white, male, and conservative Beltway voice, the series still pioneered a new approach to the nightly newscast. Like a number of other stations, Maine Public Broadcasting recently concluded its annual "Reading Rainbow Young Writers and Illustrators" contest, which encourages children to write and illustrate their own stories. And the Wisconsin Collaborative Project, aptly described by Friedland (1995: 147) as a project of the public sphere, has been acclaimed as extraordinary and useful programming.

Even with these moments of excellence and service, however, public broadcasting is an institution plagued with problems. It seems especially constructive to advance a philosophical and historical narrative about mission at a time when public media professionals and policy makers face decisions about digital spectrum use. Such a narrative demonstrates the importance of specific policy and rhetorical choices. Marilyn Lashley (1992a: 770) has shown that executive turnover in the White House caused startling policy change for public broadcasting between 1967 and 1989. Similarly, compromises, campaign strategies, and discourse choices in 1934, 1950–51, and 1967 produced a powerful, long-lasting ideological shape for public broadcasting that has narrowed its form and function.

At the same time, the arguments embedded in its discursive history position public media as an institution of public life. Visionaries past and present have believed that public broadcasting could provide a space for vigorous and reflexive discussion, enable social reform, and bind Americans together as a Public. Public television's future as an agent of the public sphere depends importantly on institutional choices that include deliberate claiming of a progressive public service identity and the cultivation of internal resolve and a broad conversation about publicness.

For years, the bell at Kansas State University's Anderson Hall ordered the daily lives of students and faculty. On December 1, 1924, the bell rang again, when KSAC radio signed on the air. As weather station 9YV became KSAC, the "Voice of Kansas State University," KSU alumni gathered around the few available radio receivers to hear the station's initial broadcast. "The story is that when these people, meeting in large halls and private homes, heard the Anderson Hall bell ringing, many started to weep, overcome by emotion" (Titus 1996). It was the emotion of memory, the remembrance of shared experiences in a common place, the goals and commitments of a collective life. The peal of the KSU bell was a call to community—a place of shared goals, history, imagination, and spaces of the mind.

This book began as a search for public media vision; it closes with a call for community and change within public television. In the final analysis, public broadcasting's ability to function as an agent of social reform, public speech, and community ties relies upon collective action. The work ahead is too hard, too expensive, at times too frustrating to do alone. As public broadcasting moves forward in the twenty-first century, it requires a powerful identity, a clear and compelling vision, and the clanging of a community bell that summons us all to old commitments. Lacking these new practices, public media will be bound to repeat the course that has compromised its public mission and institutional viability over the years.

Bibliography

"Air Enemies Unite Forces." 1934. *Variety*, May 8, 37.

"America's Forgotten Children." 2002. *Save the Children*. Online at www.savethe children.org/afc/afc_education.shtml. Accessed October 2, 2002.

Anderson, Benedict. 1983. *Imagined Communities*. London: Verso.

Andrew, John A., III. 1998. *Lyndon Johnson and the Great Society*. Chicago: Ivan R. Dee.

Arendt, Hannah. 1958. *The Human Condition*. Chicago: University of Chicago Press.

Aufderheide, Patricia. 1991. "Public Television and the Public Sphere." *Critical Studies in Mass Communication* 8:176.

Avery, Robert K. 1993. Introduction to *Public Service Broadcasting in a Multichannel Environment: The History and Survival of an Ideal*. Ed. Robert K. Avery. New York: Longman.

Avery, Robert K., and Robert Pepper. 1980. "An Institutional History of Public Broadcasting." *Journal of Communication* 30 (Summer): 126.

Bauman, John, and Thomas Coode. 1988. *In the Eye of the Great Depression: New Deal Reporters and the Agony of the American People*. DeKalb: Northern Illinois University Press.

Bedford, Karen Everhart. 1996. "Advisory Panel Seeks PBS 'Vision'—In Writing." *Current*, June 17, 1.

———. 1998. "Hume Hopes PBS Project Leads to an 'Oasis' for the Citizen." Originally published in *Current*, June 8. Online at www.current.org/el/el810d.html. Accessed May 5, 2002.

Behrens, Steve. 1996a. "In Debt, WQED Considers Divesting Second Station." *Current*, February 12, 17.

———. 1996b. "System Places Marginal Value on 'Overlaps.'" *Current*, July 22, 1, 11.

Berman, Marshall. 1982. *All That Is Solid Melts Into Air: The Experience of Modernity*. New York: Simon and Schuster.

Bitzer, Lloyd. 1968. "The Rhetorical Situation." *Philosophy and Rhetoric* 1: 3-4.

Black, Edwin. 1970. "The Second Persona." *Quarterly Journal of Speech* 56 (April): 109–19.

Black, Jay, and Jennings Bryant. 1996. *Introduction to Communication*. 4th ed. Dubuque, Iowa: Brown and Benchmark.

Blakely, Robert J. 1971. *The People's Instrument*. Washington, D.C.: Public Affairs Press.

———. 1979. *To Serve the Public Interest: Educational Broadcasting in the United States*. Syracuse, N.Y.: Syracuse University Press.

Blandenbaker, Tim. 1996. NPR National Affairs Internal memorandum, October 17.

Blumenthal, Ralph. 1995. "Giving Up One Public Station to Save Two." *New York Times*, June 6, C14.

Boddy, William. 1990. *Fifties Television: The Industry and Its Critics*. Chicago: Univeristy of Illinois Press.

Bourdieu, Pierre. 1984. *Distinction: A Social Critique of the Judgement of Taste*. Cambridge: Harvard University Press.

Brenner, Elsa. 1995. "Country's Congress Members Speak Out." *New York Times*, April 9, C1.

Briller, Bert. 1996. "Accent on Access Television." *Television Quarterly*, March, 51–58.

Brown, Carolyn. 1998. Interview by author. Iowa City, Iowa, June 5.

Brown, James A. 1989. "Struggle Against Commercialism: The 1934 'Harney Lobby' for Nonprofit Frequency Allocations." *Journal of Broadcasting and Electronic Media* 33 (Summer): 273–91.

Bullert, B. J. 1995. *Public Television: Politics and the Battle Over Documentary Film*. New Brunswick, N.J.: Rutgers University Press.

Campbell, James. 1992. *The Community Reconstructs: The Meaning of Pragmatic Social Thought*. Urbana: University of Illinois Press.

"Carlson Sees Waste in ITVS, Defends Nix on Whitewater Doc." 1996. *Current*, March 25, 8.

Carnegie Commission. 1967. *Public Television: A Program for Action*. Report and Recommendations of the Carnegie Commission on Educational Television. New York: Harper & Row.

———. 1979. *A Public Trust*. Report of the Carnegie Commission on the Future of Public Broadcasting. New York: Bantam Books.

Carter, Paul. 1983. *Another Part of the Fifties*. New York: Columbia University Press.

"Citizen-Oriented Reporting." 1996. *Current*, February 19, 6.

Cohen, Jeff, and Norman Solomon. 1995. "*MacNeil/Lehrer Newshour* at 20: Hold the Cheers." *Media Beat*, September 25, 1.

Collins, Geneva. 1999. "Public TV Seeks 'Flexibility' in Money-Making Uses of DTV." Originally published in *Current*, February 22. Online at www.current.org/dtv/dtv903a.html. Accessed May 10, 2002.

Collins, Robert M. 1994. "Growth Liberalism in the Sixties." In *The Sixties . . . From Memory to History*. Ed. David Farber. Chapel Hill: University of North Carolina Press.

Congressional Record. 1927. January 29. Washington, D.C.

Congressional Record. 1934. May 15. Washington, D.C.

Congressional Record. 1935. January 21. Washington, D.C.

Congressional Record. 1967. February 28. Washington, D.C.

Copps, Michael J. "Dissenting Statement of Commissioner Michael J. Copps." Online at www.fcc.gov/Speeches/Copps/Statements/2001/stmjc116.html. Accessed May 18, 2002.

"Corporation for Public Broadcasting." 1967. *Weekly Compilation of Presidential Documents*, February 26, 311.

Crawford, Stanley. 1986. "*Mayordomo*": *Chronicle of an "Acequia" in Northern New Mexico*. Albuquerque: University of New Mexico Press.

Curran, James. 1996. "Mass Media and Democracy Revisited." In *Mass Media and Society*. 2d ed. Ed. James Curran and Michael Gurevitch. London: Arnold.

Daniel, Jamie Owen. 1997. "Does 'Poetry Make Nothing Happen?': The Case for Public Poetry as a Counter-Public Sphere." Paper presented at Conference on Contemporary Poetry: Poetry and the Public Sphere, at Rutgers University, New Brunswick, N.J., April 27.

Daressa, Lawrence. 1990. "Does the Public Have a Future in Public Television?" Speech presented at the Center for Communication colloquium, December 14, New York, N.Y.

———. 1996. "Television for a Change: To Help Us Change Ourselves." *Current*, February 12, 20.

Day, James. 1995. *The Vanishing Vision: The Inside Story of Public Television*. Berkeley: University of California Press.

"A Declaration of Principles." 1980. *PTR*, May/June, 10.

Dewey, John. 1900. *The School and Society*. Chicago: University of Chicago Press.

———. 1927. *The Public and Its Problems*. New York: Holt.

———. 1931. *The Way Out of Educational Confusion*. Cambridge: Harvard University Press.

Diamond, Sigmund. 1992. *Compromised Campus: The Collaboration of Universities with the Intelligence Community, 1945–1955*. New York: Oxford University Press.

"Dropout Rates." 2002. Child Trends Data Bank. Online at www.childtrends databand.org/eduskills/attendance/HighSchoolDropout.htm. Accessed October 1, 2002.

Durr, Clifford J. Papers. LPR 25, box 36, folder 4. Alabama State Archives, Montgomery, Ala. Used by permission of the State of Alabama.

Early, Stephen. 1936. Memorandum to the chair of the FCC, February 4. OF2001, Radio Station WLWL (NYC) 1936. Franklin D. Roosevelt Library Archives, Hyde Park, N.Y. Used by permission of the Franklin and Eleanor Roosevelt Institute.

Edwards, Ellen. 1995a. "Pressler Wants Public Media to Go Public." *Washington Post*, January 24, A1.

———. 1995b. "Gingrich Vows to Zero Out CPB." *Washington Post*, February 17, C1.

———. 1995c. "Al Gore Speaks Out for Public Television." *Washington Post*, March 3, C1, C4.

Edwards, Ellen, and Mike Mills. 1995. "'Vultures' Circle Public TV." *Washington Post*, January 24, C1.

Edwards, Ellen, and Jacqueline Trescott. 1995. "Budget Ax Falls on Arts, Public TV." *Washington Post*, February 23, C1.

Engelman, Ralph. 1990. "The Origins of Public Access Cable Television, 1966–1972." *Journalism Monographs* 123 (October): 3–4.

———. 1996. *Public Radio and Television in America: A Political History.* London: Sage.

"Escalation by Whatever Name." 1967. *New York Times*, February 28.

Evans, Sara, and Harry Boyte. 1992. *Free Spaces: The Sources of Democratic Change in America.* Chicago: University of Chicago Press.

Ewen, Stewart. 1996. *PR! A Social History of Spin.* New York: Basic Books.

FAIR [Fairness and Accuracy in Reporting]. 1990. "All the Usual Suspects: The *MacNeil/Lehrer NewsHour* and *Nightline*." May 21.

Farhi, Paul. 1995. "Big Bird Taken Off Death Row." *Washington Post*, July 13, C1.

FCC allocations hearings, 1949–50. Ohio State University Archives, Columbus. Used by permission of Ohio State University.

Fletcher, C. Scott. Papers. National Public Broadcasting Archives, Hornbake Library, University of Maryland, College Park. Used by permission of the University of Maryland Libraries.

———. 1957. Introduction to *Toward the Liberally Educated Executive.* Ed. Robert A. Goldwin. White Plains, N.Y.: Fund for Adult Education.

Fletcher, C. Scott. 1973. Interview by Charles T. Morrissey. March 1. Fletcher Papers, series 1, box 1, folders 5 and 6.

Ford Foundation. 1952. *The Whole Town's Talking: Runnells, Iowa.* Television program. Dir. Charles Guggenheim. Ames, Iowa: WOI-TV.

———. 1961. *1951–1961: A Ten Year Report of the Fund for Adult Education.* White Plains, N.Y.: Ford Foundation.

Fraser, Nancy. 1993. "Rethinking the Public Sphere: A Contribution to the Critique of Actually Existing Democracy." In *Habermas and the Public Sphere*. Ed. Craig Calhoun. Cambridge, Mass: MIT Press.

Friedland, Lewis A. 1995. "Public Television as Public Sphere: The Case of the Wisconsin Collaborative Project." *Journal of Broadcasting and Electronic Media* 39 (Spring): 147.

Giles, Robert. 1998. Introduction. *Media Studies Journal: "1968"* (Fall): xi.

Gray, Jerry. 1995. "House Committee Discusses Public Broadcasting Budget." *New York Times*, January 20, A22.

Griffin, Cindy. 1996. "The Essentialist Roots of the Public Sphere: A Feminist Critique." *Western Journal of Communication* 60 (Winter): 21–23.

Guggenheim, Charles. 1996. Speech at University of Iowa Communication Studies Department, Iowa City, Iowa, October.

Gunn, Hartford. 1980. "A Proposal for Multiple Program Services in Public Television." *PTR*, May/June, 37–44.

Habermas, Jürgen. 1989. *The Structural Transformation of the Public Sphere: An Inquiry Into a Category of Bourgeois Society*. Cambridge: MIT Press.

Hall, Jane. 1997. "Is BBC's New Cable Deal a Threat to PBS?" *The Seattle Times*, November 10, at www.seattletimes.com/extra/browse. Accessed November 25, 1998.

Halonen, Doug. 1999. "Public Says TV Should Do More." *Electronic Media* 18, no. 3: 108.

"Hanley Suggests a New Deal." 1934. *New York Times*, May 13, 7.

Hartzell, Dick, R. F. Smith, and Walter Bernanek. n.d. "Television and An American Town." WOI Radio and Television Files. 5/6/4, box 5. Iowa State University Archives, Ames, Iowa. Used by permission of Iowa State University.

Henderson, Vivian. 1970. "Meeting the Tastes, Needs and Desires of the Black Community." *Educational Broadcasting Review* 4:29.

Hennock, Freida B. Papers. Harry S. Truman Library Archives, Harry S. Truman Presidential Library, Independence, Mo. Used by permission of the Harry S. Truman Presidential Library.

Hill, Frank Ernest. 1942. *Tune In for Education: Eleven Years of Education by Radio*. New York: National Committee on Education by Radio.

Hoynes, William. 1994. *Public Television for Sale: Media, the Market, and the Public Sphere*. Boulder, Colo.: Westview Press.

Huesca, Robert. 2001. "And Now Reporting Live . . . the People Themselves." *Newsday*, August 19, B8.

Huff, Richard. 2001. "Chs. 13 and 21 Plan to Merge Operations." *Daily News*, August 1, 67.

Hurlbert, Raymond. 1981. Interview by Jim Robertson. March 4. Robertson Papers, box 2. National Public Broadcasting Archives, Hornbake Library, University of Maryland, College Park. Used by permission of the University of Maryland Libraries.

Hull, Richard B. Private Papers. Iowa State University Archives, Iowa State University, Ames, Iowa. Used by permission of Iowa State University.
———. 1950. Letter to Senator Edwin C. Johnson. June 19. NAEB, box 19, folder 1. Wisconsin State Historical Society Archives, University of Wisconsin, Madison, Wis. Used by permission of University of Wisconsin.
"Hume Will Be 'Choreographer' of Democracy Project." 1996. Current, April 22, 18.
Husband, Charles. 1996. "The Right to Be Understood: Conceiving the Multi-Ethnic Public Sphere." Innovation: The European Journal of Social Sciences 9, no. 2: 205–10.
"If Ben Kubasik Calls, Be Sure to Listen to Him." 1967. Chicago Sun Times, July 19, 8.
JCET allocations hearings, 1949–51. Ohio State University Archives, Columbus. Used by permission of Ohio State University.
Jensen, Elizabeth. 2002. "A Network's Mastery Has Gone to Pieces." Los Angeles Times, May 12, A1.
Johnson, Nicholas. 1968. "Soul Music Is Not Enough." Address at Annual Television and Radio Announcers Convention, August 17, Miami, Fla.
Joint Committee on Educational Television (JCET). Educational Television. (RG 40/62/5), "JCET: Meetings, Reports: 1953 (Folder 2 of 2)." I. Keith Tyler Papers. Ohio State University Archives, Columbus. Used by permission of Ohio State University.
Josephson Institute of Ethics. 2001. "The Ethics of American Youth: 2000 Report Card." Online at www.josephsoninstitute.org/Survey2000/violence2000-commentary.htm. Accessed February 4, 2002.
Kellner, Douglas. 1990. Television and the Crisis of Democracy. Boulder, Colo.: Westview Press.
———. 2001. "Intellectuals, the New Public Sphere, and Techno-Politics." Illuminations: The Critical Theory Website, October. Online at www.gseis.ucla.edu/courses/ed253a/newDK/intell.htm. Accessed May 13, 2002.
Kloppenberg, James. Uncertain Victory: Social Democracy and Progressivism in European and American Thought, 1870-1920. New York: Oxford University Press, 1986.
Kolbert, Elizabeth. 1995. "The President of PBS Waxes Eloquent in Its Cause." New York Times, June 26, C1.
Kozol, Jonathan. 1967. Death at an Early Age: The Destruction of the Hearts and Minds of Negro Children in the Boston Public Schools. Boston: Houghlin Mifflin.
———. 1998. "Principals, Grandmothers, and Resiliency." Education Digest 63, Issue 6 (February): 20-23
———. 1991. Savage Inequalities: Children in American Schools. New York: HarperCollins.
Lagemann, Ellen Condliffe. 1992. The Politics of Knowledge: The Carnegie Corporation, Philanthropy, and Public Policy. Chicago: University of Chicago Press.

Lashley, Marilyn. 1992a. "Even in Public Television, Ownership Changes Matter." *Communication Research* 19 (December): 770.

———. 1992b. *Public Television: Panacea, Pork Barrel, or Public Trust.* New York: Greenwood Press.

Lazarsfeld, Paul. 1949. "Radio Seminar 1949." July 2. Speech. Series Record 13/5/1, box 4. University of Illinois Archives, Urbana-Champaign. Used by permission of University of Illinois.

Leach, Eugene E. 1983. *Tuning Out Education: The Cooperation Doctrine in Radio, 1922–38.* Washington, D.C.: Current.

Ledbetter, James. 1997. "PBS Strikes Labor." *Nation*, June 30, 6.

Lee, Ivy. Private Papers. Princeton University Archives, Seeley G. Mudd Library, Princeton University, Princeton, N.J. Used by permission of the Princeton University Libraries.

Levine, Rhonda. 1988. *Class Struggle and the New Deal: Industrial Labor, Industrial Capital, and the State.* Lawrence: University of Kansas Press.

Lewis, Philip. 1961. *Educational Television Guidebook.* New York: McGraw Hill.

Lowell, Ralph. 1968. Letter to Thomas Hoving. C. Scott Fletcher Papers, Box 7, "Miscellaneous Correspondence," November 4. National Public Broadcasting Archives. University of Maryland, College Park. Used by permission of the University of Maryland Libraries.

Maloney, Martin. 1969. "A Philosophy of Educational Television." In *The Farther Vision: Educational Television Today.* Ed. Allen E. Koenig and Ruane B. Hill. Madison: University of Wisconsin Press.

Martin, Christopher R. 1999. "Assessing Public Journalism." *Journal of Communication* 49:160.

May, Elaine Tyler. 1988. *Homeward Bound: American Families in the Cold War Era.* New York: Basic Books.

———. 1989. "Explosive Issues: Sex, Women, and the Bomb." In *Recasting America: Culture and Politics in the Age of Cold War.* Ed. Lary May. Chicago: University of Chicago Press.

McChesney, Robert W. 1987. "Crusade Against Mammon: Father Harney, WLWL, and the Debate over Radio in the 1930s." *Journalism History* 14, No. 4 (Winter): 4.

———. 1993. *Telecommunications, Mass Media, and Democracy: The Battle for the Control of U.S. Broadcasting, 1928–1935.* New York: Oxford University Press.

———. 1999. *Rich Media, Poor Democracy: Communication Politics in Dubious Times.* Urbana-Champaign: University of Illinois Press.

———. 2001. "Policing the Thinkable." *Open Democracy: Thinking for Our Time*, October 25. Online at www.opendemocracy.net/forum. Accessed May 21, 2002.

McCourt, Thomas. 1996. "National Public Radio and the Rationalization of the Public." Ph.D. diss. University of Texas.

McElvaine, Robert. 1993. *The Great Depression: America 1929–1941*. New York: Times Books.

Mertz, Paul. 1978. *New Deal Policy and Southern Rural Poverty*. Baton Rouge: Louisiana State University Press.

Minnow, Newton. 1993. Foreword to *Public Service Broadcasting in a Multi-channel Environment: The History and Survival of an Ideal*. Ed. Robert K. Avery. New York: Longman.

"National Education News." 2000. *Ed.Net Briefs*. Online at www.edbriefs.com/usa00-01/12.18.00usa.html. Accessed October 2, 2002.

Negt, Oskar, and Alexander Kluge. 1993. *Public Sphere and Experience: Toward an Analysis of the Bourgeois and Proletarian Public Sphere*. Trans. Peter Labanyi. Minneapolis: University of Minnesota Press.

Nelson, Anne. 1995. "Public Broadcasting: Free at Last?" *Columbia Journalism Review* 34 (November/December): 16-19.

Newman, Richard. 2001. "Sponsor's Significant Other: Chubb Values Its Tie to 'Antiques Roadshow.'" *Bergen County Record*, July 27, B1.

Noelle-Newmann, Elisabeth. 1974. "The Spiral of Silence: A Theory of Public Opinion." *Journal of Communication* 24, No. 2 (Spring): 43–51.

Odenwald, Dan. 2001. "FCC Okays Revenue Services in Digital TV Bitstream." *Current*, October 22, 1, 3.

Paley, William. 1934. "Statement to the FCC." Ivy Lee Private Papers. Box 57. Princeton University Archives. Used by permission of Princeton University, Princeton, N.J.

Paulu, Burton. n.d. "The Challenge of the 242 Channels." (RG 40/62/5), "JCET: Meetings, Reports: 1953 (Folder 2 of 2)." I. Keith Tyler Papers. Ohio State University Archives, Columbus. Used by permission of Ohio State University.

"PBS Democracy Project Wins Angel Award." 1997. Press release, March 4, at www.pbs.org/insidepbs/news/angel/html. Accessed September 14, 1998.

Pearce, W. Barnett, and Stephen W. Littlejohn. 1997. *Moral Conflict: When Social Worlds Collide*. Thousand Oaks, Calif.: Sage.

Poster, Mark. 1995. "CyberDemocracy: Internet and the Public Sphere." Online at www.humanities.uci.edu/mposter/writing/democ.html. Accessed January 20, 2002.

Powell, Clyde. 1997. Interview by author. Portales, N. Mex., December 21.

President's Papers, 1921–22. Kansas State University, 44-a. Kansas State University Archives, Manhattan, Kans. Used by permission of Kansas State University.

"Producers Reject Proposed Public TV 'Czar.'" 1989. *Broadcasting*, October, 53.

"PTV: Pluralistic Society with Reduced Allegiances." 1996. *Current*, November 11, 17.

Public Broadcasting Service (PBS). 1996a. "Funding History of the Corporation for Public Broadcasting." Report. May.

———. 1996b. "Appropriations Summary of Specific Programs Affecting Public Television." Memorandum. June.

———. 1996c. *Public Broadcasting Service: An Overview*. Report. July.

———. 1996d. "Public Television Income by Source." Memorandum. August.

"Public Television Stations in the Digital Age." 2002. Online at www.fcc.gov/mmb/prd/dtv/ncdtv.html. February 12. Accessed April 21, 2002.

Quinn, Robert. 1967. Letter to Thomas Hoving. June 2. Fletcher Papers, box 6.

Ramos, Victor Manuel. 2001. "Trustee Quits Over Ch. 21 Merger Plan." *Newsday*, July 31, A3.

Rathbun, Elizabeth. 1995. "Poll Heightens Politics of PBS Funding Debate." *Broadcasting and Cable*, January 23, 164.

"Renovating Democracy's Feedback Loops." 1996. *Current*, February 19, 1.

Richards, Sandra L. 1993. "Caught in the Act of Social Definition: On the Road with Anna Deavere Smith." In *Acting Out: Feminist Performances*. Ed. Lynda Hart and Peggy Phelan. Ann Arbor: University of Michigan Press.

Robertson, Anne. 1998. "Staying in School Makes Sense." June 20, at npin.org.pnewn96/pnewn96I.html. Accessed January 15, 1999.

Robinson, Ira. 1930. "Educational Obligations of the Broadcaster." In *Education on the Air: First Yearbook of the Institute for Education by Radio*. Columbus: Ohio State University Press.

Rockefeller Foundation Papers. Rockefeller Foundation Archives, Rockefeller Archive Center, North Tarrytown, N.Y. Used by permission of the Rockefeller Archive Center.

Rowland, Williard D., Jr. 1993. "Public Service Broadcasting in the United States: Its Mandate, Institutions, and Conflicts." In *Public Service Broadcasting in a Multichannel Environment: The History and Survival of an Ideal*. Ed. Robert K. Avery. New York: Longman.

Ryan, Duane. 1997. Interview by author. Portales, N. Mex., March 15.

Schaffer, Jan. 1997. "Civic Journalism: The Idea, The Evolution, The Impact." *Pew Center for Civic Journalism*, November 20, at www.pewcenter.org.s-wiseman.html. Accessed November 20, 1998.

Schmeckebier, Laurence. 1932. *The Federal Radio Commission: Its History, Activities, and Organization*. Washington, D.C.: Brookings Institution.

Schramm, Wilbur. 1962. "A National Policy for Educational Television." In *ETV: The Next Ten Years*. Stanford, Calif.: Stanford University Institute for Communication Research.

Sennett, Richard. 1974. *The Fall of Public Man*. New York: Knopf.

Shales, Tom. 1995. "The Misguided Missiles Aimed at Public TV." *Washington Post*, February 27, B1.

Sitkoff, Harvard. 1985. *Fifty Years Later: The New Deal Evaluated.* New York: Knopf.

Smulyan, Susan. 1994. *Selling Radio: The Commercialization of American Broadcasting, 1920–1934.* Washington, D.C.: Smithsonian Institution Press.

"Station Execs Discuss DTV Revenue Potential." 1999. Originally published in *Current,* January 25. Online at www.current.org/dtv/dtv903a.html. Accessed May 15, 2002.

Stone, I. F. 1963. *The Haunted Fifties: 1953–1963.* Boston: Little, Brown.

Sucherman, Stuart. 1987. "Old Enough to Get Its Act Together." *Channels,* October, 68.

"Suicide in the United States." 2002. Center for Disease Control. October 1. Online at www.cdc.gov/ncipc/factsheets/suifacts.htm. Accessed October 2, 2002.

"12 Groups Join Forces, Will Seek Educational Video." 1953. Memorandum. May 3. Hulbert Papers, 23.1.1.1.1. Birmingham Public Library Archives, Birmingham, Ala. Used by permission of the City of Birmingham.

Titus, Ralph. 1996. Interview by author. Manhatten, Kansas, July 18.

Twentieth Century Fund. 1993. *Quality Time?* Report of the Twentieth Century Fund Task Force on Public Television. New York: Twentieth Century Fund Press.

Tyler, I. Keith. 1981. Interview by Jim Robertson. August 21. I. Keith Tyler Papers, RG 40/62, Accession #173/94. Ohio State University Archives, Columbus. Used by permission of Ohio State University.

Tyler, Tracy. 1933. *An Appraisal of Radio Broadcasting in the Land-Grant Colleges and State Universities.* Washington, D.C.: National Committee on Education by Radio.

"U.S. Radio System Scored and Lauded at Educators' Meet." 1934. *Broadcasting,* May 15, 16.

U.S. Senate. 1943. Committee on Interstate Commerce. *Hearings on S. 2910.* March. Washington: GPO, 1934.

Wagner, Robert. Private Papers. LE box 223, folders 1489–90. Georgetown University Archives, Washington, D.C. Used by permission of the Georgetown University Libraries.

Welling, Joseph. 1996. "Values Beget Institutions, Which Beget Programs." *Current,* February 12, 21.

Will, George. 1995. "Give Them the Ax." *Washington Post,* January 8, C1.

Williams, Raymond. 1958. *Culture and Society: 1780–1950.* New York: Columbia University Press.

Witcover, Jules. 1998. "Reassessing the Winners and Losers: A Reporter Looks Back at the Events He Covered in 1968." *Media Studies Journal: "1968"* (Fall): 21.

Index

151

About the Author

Glenda R. Balas is an assistant professor of communication and journalism at the University of New Mexico, Albuquerque. She received a Ph.D. in communication studies from the University of Iowa in 1999. Dr. Balas worked for more than a decade in U.S. public television, and much of her work as a media scholar focuses on the potential and practice of public service media.